P9-DGE-747

Too Cute!
Plastic Canvas™

Edited by Vicki Blizzard

HOUSE of
WHITE
BIRCHES

PUBLISHERS
SINCE 1947

Too Cute!
Plastic Canvas™

Copyright © 2003 House of White Birches,
Berne, Indiana 46711

Editor: Vicki Blizzard
Managing Editor: Kelly Keim
Technical Editor: June Sprunger
Copy Editor: Mary Martin
Technical Artists: Liz Morgan, Mitch Moss,
Travis Spangler, Chad Summers

Photography: Jeff Chilcote, Tammy Christian, Christena Green,
Kelly Heydinger, Shane Piquignot, Nancy Sharp, Justin Wiard
Photography Assistant: Linda Quinlan

Publishing Services Manager: Brenda Gallmeyer
Graphic Arts Supervisor: Ronda Bechinski
Book and Cover Design: Jessi Butler
Graphic Artist: Amy S. Lin
Production Assistants: Janet Bowers, Marj Morgan
Traffic Coordinator: Sandra Beres

Chief Executive Officer: John Robinson
Publishing Marketing Director: David McKee
Book Marketing Manager: Craig Scott
Product Development Director: Vivian Rothe
Publishing Services Director: Brenda R. Wendling

Printed in the United States of America
First Printing: 2003
Library of Congress Number: 2001097999
ISBN: 1-882138-97-X

A Warm Welcome
From the Editor

Dear Stitching Friends,

Have you ever seen a plastic canvas design that makes you say, "That is just *too cute!*"? If so, then you're sure to love this collection of adorable projects!

Sweet angels, cuddly animals, whimsical Christmas characters, sunny flowers and many more friends are waiting for you to stitch and share them with those you love!

Our "too cute" characters will fill your home with whimsical charm as they decorate tissue boxes, coasters, ornaments, magnets and so much more. They're also perfect for giving gifts of cheer or selling at bazaars—who can resist their sunny smiles and endearing faces?

So get ready to spread a little sunshine by stitching these delightful plastic canvas projects to dress up your home!

Warm regards,

Vicki Blizzard

Contents
Spring Fling

Summer Sparkles

³⁄₈-inch loop; secure ends with a dab of glue.

3. Using yellow throughout and starting at bottom edges, Whipstitch purse sides to side edges of purse front and back, then continue Whipstitching front and back together up to handle. Whipstitch bottom to front, sides and back.

4. Using red, Whipstitch straight edge of purse flap to purse along Whipstitch line on back, working through all thicknesses.

5. For bow, cut three 1-inch lengths and one 6-inch length of ribbon. For tails, cut an inverted "V" on one end of two 1-inch lengths. Make a loop with 6-inch length and wrap remaining 1-inch length around center of loop, gluing on backside; glue tails and loop to flap.

6. Glue flat braid around bottom of purse, clipping corners and easing as necessary to fit. Center and glue red

felt to bottom of purse.

7. Wrap dragonfly wire around toothpick to curl, leaving bottom ½ inch straight. Insert bottom of wire under stitching along side of purse.

8. Glue one assembled small daisy to bottom left corner of purse front.

Hat Assembly

1. For box bottom, using yellow, Whipstitch ends of inner hatband together, forming a circle, then Overcast top edge. Whipstitch bottom edge to blue Whipstitch line on hat brim.

2. Glue flat braid around outer edge of hat brim, easing to fit as necessary. Glue yellow felt circle to bottom of hat brim.

3. For box lid, Whipstitch top edge of outer hatband to hat top.

4. Glue a 12½-inch length of ribbon around hatband, overlapping in back. Make a multiloop bow by wrapping a 23-inch length of ribbon around fingers three times. Secure center of loops with thin wire, and arrange loops as desired; cut excess wire.

5. Glue bow over ribbon overlap in back. Glue assembled large daisy over center of bow, then glue artificial flowers on both sides of bow.

6. Spacing evenly, glue assembled small daisies around hat band.

7. For dragonfly, follow step 7 of purse assembly, then insert straight end of wire under stitching on hatband behind bow.

8. Place box lid over inner hatband on box bottom. ✄

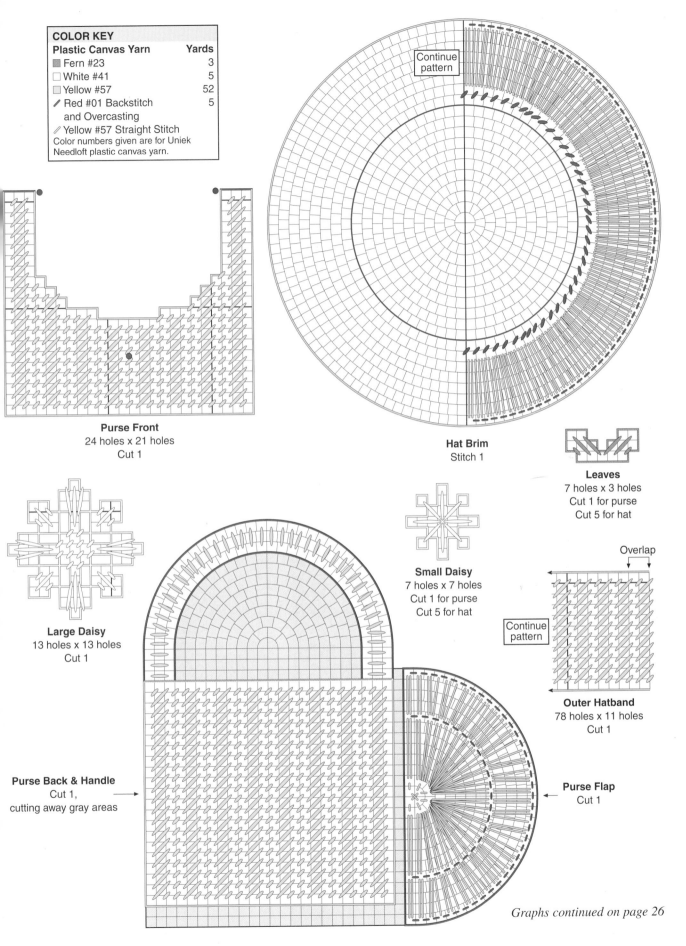

COLOR KEY

Plastic Canvas Yarn	Yards
■ Fern #23	3
□ White #41	5
□ Yellow #57	52
✎ Red #01 Backstitch and Overcasting	5
✎ Yellow #57 Straight Stitch	

Color numbers given are for Uniek Needloft plastic canvas yarn.

Purse Front
24 holes x 21 holes
Cut 1

Continue pattern

Hat Brim
Stitch 1

Leaves
7 holes x 3 holes
Cut 1 for purse
Cut 5 for hat

Large Daisy
13 holes x 13 holes
Cut 1

Small Daisy
7 holes x 7 holes
Cut 1 for purse
Cut 5 for hat

Overlap

Continue pattern

Outer Hatband
78 holes x 11 holes
Cut 1

Purse Back & Handle
Cut 1,
cutting away gray areas

Purse Flap
Cut 1

Graphs continued on page 26

Gift Bear

Skill Level

Intermediate

Size

6⅛ inches W x
7½ inches H x
2 inches D

Say "I love you" by stitching and giving this precious bear. He comes complete with a decorated box for tiny trinkets and a miniature greeting card.

Design by
Ronda Bryce

Materials

- 2 sheets almond 7-count plastic canvas
- 4 (3-inch) plastic canvas radial circles
- Coats & Clark Red Heart Misty chunky weight yarn Art. E712 as listed in color key
- Uniek Needloft plastic canvas yarn as listed in color key
- DMC 6-strand embroidery floss as listed in color key
- #16 tapestry needle
- 26 (5mm) ivory pearl beads
- 9 inches (⅛-inch-wide) light pink lace
- Hand-sewing needle and ivory sewing thread

Bear

1. Cut bear from plastic canvas according to graph (page 16). Cut two 7-hole x 22-hole pieces for arms and two 10-hole x 28-hole pieces for legs.

2. Stitch arms and legs with Aran Continental Stitches. Whipstitch short ends of each piece together to form four cylinders. Overcast one end of each cylinder with Aran.

3. Stitch and Overcast bear, working uncoded areas with Aran Continental Stitches. Using sewing needle and ivory thread, attach beads to ears where indicated.

4. When background stitching is completed, Straight Stitch leaves with fern and work French Knot flowers with pink.

5. For paws on arms, cut the six outermost rows of holes from two 3-inch radial circles. Using lavender, work a Straight Stitch from each hole on the outermost row of holes to center of circle. Work a Cross Stitch in center, then stitch an ivory bead over Cross Stitch with sewing needle and ivory thread.

6. Repeat step 5 for paws on legs, cutting the five outermost rows of holes from remaining two radial circles.

7. Using Aran throughout, Whipstitch paws to corresponding arms and legs. Tack arms and legs to bear as in photo.

Gift Box

1. Cut gift box pieces and heart according to graphs (pages 16).

2. Stitch box pieces following graphs. Stitch and Overcast heart, working uncoded area with Aran Continental Stitches.

3. When background stitching is completed, work fern Straight Stitches and pink French Knots on heart, then add ivory bead where indicated with sewing needle and ivory thread.

4. Using lavender throughout, Whipstitch front and back to sides, then Whipstitch front, back and sides to bottom. Overcast top edges of front and sides; Overcast lid around side and front edges. Whipstitch back edge of lid to top edge of box back.

5. For box closure, using sewing needle and ivory thread, sew pearl to front where indicated on graph. Add a corresponding loop of lavender yarn to center front edge of lid.

6. Using sewing needle and ivory thread, sew lace around edge of heart, then sew heart to front of box.

Envelope & Note

1. Cut plastic canvas according to graphs (page 16).

2. Stitch and Overcast note, then work lettering with very light ash gray embroidery floss.

3. Stitch uncoded envelope pieces with Aran Continental Stitches. Work fern Straight Stitches and pink French Knot when background stitching is completed.

4. Overcast top edge of envelope front. With right sides facing front, place envelope front on envelope back, aligning bottom and side edges; Whipstitch together, then Overcast remaining edges of envelope back.

Finishing

1. Using photo as a guide throughout, insert note in envelope. Tack envelope to bear's arm with sewing needle and ivory thread.

2. Set gift box between bear's paws. ✄

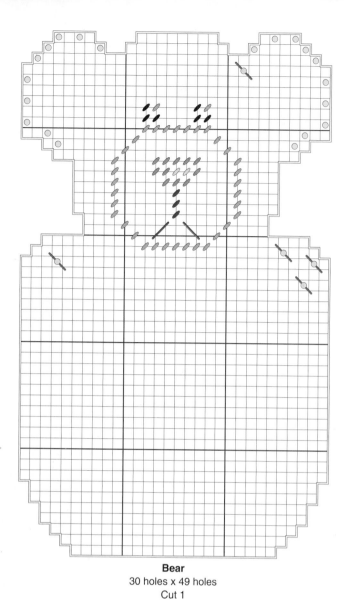

Bear
30 holes x 49 holes
Cut 1

Gift Box Front & Back
13 holes x 16 holes
Cut 2

Gift Box Side
10 holes x 16 holes
Cut 2

Envelope Front
15 holes x 6 holes
Cut 1

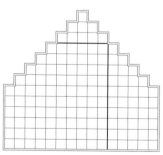

Envelope Back
15 holes x 13 holes
Cut 1

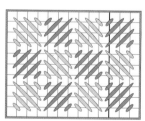

Gift Box Lid & Bottom
13 holes x 10 holes
Cut 2

Heart
11 holes x 10 holes
Cut 1

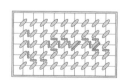

Note
10 holes x 6 holes
Cut 1

Cottage Planter

Skill Level
Advanced

Size
6¼ inches W x
6½ inches H x
6¾ inches D

Create a beautiful centerpiece with this enchanting cottage planter holding a pretty flowering treasure! Coordinating Cottage Clip appears on page 23.

Design by
Janelle Giese

Materials

- 3½ sheets clear stiff 7-count plastic canvas
- Small amount almond 7-count plastic canvas
- Uniek Needloft plastic canvas yarn as listed in color key
- DMC #3 pearl cotton as listed in color key
- DMC #5 pearl cotton as listed in color key
- #16 tapestry needle
- Tiny purchased posies
- Mill Hill Products ceramic cat with bow button #86101 from Gay Bowles Sales Inc.
- 6 inches 1½-inch-wide ivory flat lace trim
- 4-inch plant pot with attached saucer of same size
- Thick white glue

Cutting

1. Cut trellis from almond plastic canvas according to graph (page 22), cutting away blue lines. Trellis will remain unstitched.

2. Cut four 33-hole x 6-hole pieces for floor supports, four 2-hole x 3-hole pieces for window box sides and two 2-hole x 9-hole pieces for window box bases from clear stiff plastic canvas. Floor supports will remain unstitched.

3. Cut remaining pieces from clear stiff plastic canvas according to graphs (pages 19, 20, 21 and 22). Do not stitch door frame and window frame pieces.

4. Cut lace trim into four 1½-inch-wide pieces.

Walls & Window Boxes

1. Follow graphs carefully throughout all stitching and assembly. *Note: Do not stitch red, yellow and blue Whipstitch lines at this time.* Stitch cottage walls, working uncoded areas on cottage foundation with silver Continental Stitches, but do not stitch area indicated on foundation area of front wall.

2. Place both door frame pieces together and align with red lines around door on front wall. Working through all thicknesses, Whipstitch together with eggshell along outer edge and beige along inner edge.

3. Place one window frame over each window, aligning outer edge with red Whipstitch lines; Whipstitch together following instructions in step 2 for door frame. For center bars in each window, Overcast top edge with eggshell and bottom edge with beige.

4. Embroider door, Backstitching window with #5 pearl cotton. Use a full strand yarn to work French Knot roses, wrapping yarn around needle two times.

5. Continental Stitch window box sides and bases with beige. Stitch window box fronts, using a full strand yarn to Straight Stitch flowers and leaves when background stitching is completed.

6. For each window box, Whipstitch one side to each end of a base, then Whipstitch sides and base to one box front; Overcast top edges. Align window boxes with yellow Whipstitch lines under windows on cottage front, then Whipstitch together with beige.

7. Whipstitch walls together, skipping over sail blue edges at this time. Work lilac French Knots on flowered bush, wrapping yarn one time around needle.

Roof & Overhang

1. Stitch roof and roof trim pieces, Straight Stitching leaves with a full strand of yarn on trim pieces when background stitching is completed.

2. Whipstitch bottom edge of one roof piece to top edge of one trim piece to form one side of roof. Repeat with remaining pieces. Whipstitch sides together; Overcast top and bottom edges.

3. Place two Overhang pieces together and stitch as one. Overcast outside edge, leaving inside edge unworked at this time.

Floor

1. Work floor with sail blue Continental Stitches, leaving blue Whipstitch lines unworked.

2. Matching edges, place floor supports together in two sets of two. Using sail blue Continental Stitches, Whipstitch long edge of one set to wrong side of floor along one Whipstitch line of floor. Repeat, Whipstitching remaining set to floor along second Whipstitch line.

3. With floor supports on bottom, place floor inside cottage, then Whipstitch floor edges to walls along blue Whipstitch lines only, using indicated colors on coded areas and sail blue on remaining areas.

Trellis

1. Place trellis over Continental Stitches on left wall as indicated, aligning bottom edges. Following embroidery diagram, attach trellis to wall, beginning with hunter green pearl cotton Straight Stitches.

2. Continue embroidery, using only 1 ply to work forest green Straight Stitches. *Note: Some stitches will be worked on the wall next to the trellis as indicated on diagram.*

3. Use a full strand pink to work French Knot flowers, wrapping yarn around needle two times.

Porch and Base

1. Stitch porch top, side, and step riser and tread pieces, working uncoded areas with silver Continental Stitches.

2. Place both base pieces together and stitch as one, working grass on front corners of base with moss.

3. Whipstitch step and risers together, forming one long piece, then Whipstitch front edge of porch to top edge of top riser. Whipstitch porch sides to assembled steps and porch.

4. Using gray and working through all thicknesses throughout, Whipstitch back edge of porch sides to floor supports and front wall along vertical yellow Whipstitch lines. Whipstitch back edge of porch top to cottage floor and to front wall along horizontal yellow Whipstitch line.

Final Assembly

1. Using moss, Whipstitch bottom edge of front wall to base along horizontal green Whipstitch line. Using Continental Stitches, Whipstitch floor supports to back wall along yellow Whipstitch lines, using colors indicated.

2. Use moss through step 3. Beginning at front and stitching both lines alternately, Whipstitch bottom edge of porch sides and floor supports to base along green Whipstitch lines. *Note: By working lines alternately, it allows you to flip up back of base to handle needle.*

3. Whipstitch bottom edge of front riser and remaining walls of cottage to base, catching bottom edge of trellis on left wall and Overcasting grass area on front corners while Whipstitching.

4. Using beige, Whipstitch inside edges of overhang to top edges of cottage walls.

5. Using photo as a guide throughout, glue posies and short lengths of forest yarn in window boxes. Glue cat button to bottom step.

6. Glue lace trim behind windows. *Note: Bottom edges of trim will show through bottom of window.*

7. Slide cottage roof over overhang, allowing Whipstitched edge of roof and roof trim to rest on outer edge of overhang. ✄

COLOR KEY	
Plastic Canvas Yarn	**Yards**
▨ Lavender #05	2
☐ Pink #07	1
■ Brown #15	1
▨ Moss #25	11
■ Christmas green #28	5
■ Forest #29	3
▨ Sail blue #35	26
▨ Baby blue #36	27
▨ Gray #38	8
☐ Eggshell #39	23
▨ Beige #40	29
Uncoded areas are silver #37	
Continental Stitches	8
╱ Lavender #05 Straight Stitch	
╱ Pink #07 Straight Stitch	
╱ Moss #25 Straight Stitch	
╱ Forest #29 Straight Stitch	
● Lavender #05 French Knot	
○ Pink #07 French Knot	
● Lilac #45 French Knot	1
#3 Pearl Cotton	
╱ Hunter green #3346 Straight Stitch	1
#5 Pearl Cotton	
╱ Ultra dark beaver gray #844 Backstitch	1
Color numbers given are for Uniek Needloft plastic canvas yarn and DMC #3 and #5 pearl cotton.	

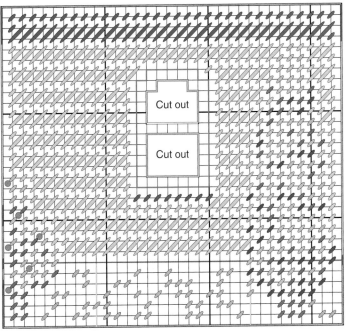

Cottage Back Wall
33 holes x 30 holes
Cut 1 from clear stiff

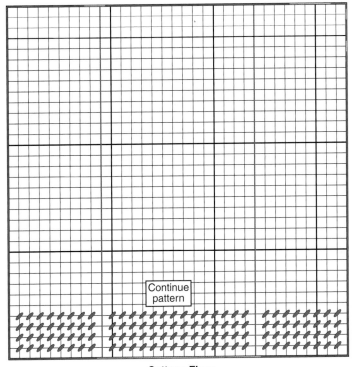

Cottage Floor
33 holes x 33 holes
Cut 1 from clear stiff

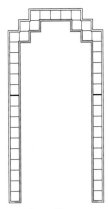

Door Frame
9 holes x 18 holes
Cut 2 from clear stiff
Do not stitch

COLOR KEY

Plastic Canvas Yarn	Yards
■ Lavender #05	2
□ Pink #07	1
■ Brown #15	1
■ Moss #25	11
■ Christmas green #28	5
■ Forest #29	3
■ Sail blue #35	26
□ Baby blue #36	27
■ Gray #38	8
□ Eggshell #39	23
■ Beige #40	29
Uncoded areas are silver #37	
Continental Stitches	8
╱ Lavender #05 Straight Stitch	
╱ Pink #07 Straight Stitch	
╱ Moss #25 Straight Stitch	
╱ Forest #29 Straight Stitch	
● Lavender #05 French Knot	
○ Pink #07 French Knot	
● Lilac #45 French Knot	1
#3 Pearl Cotton	
╱ Hunter green #3346 Straight Stitch	1
#5 Pearl Cotton	
╱ Ultra dark beaver gray	
#844 Backstitch	1

Color numbers given are for Uniek Needloft plastic canvas yarn and DMC #3 and #5 pearl cotton.

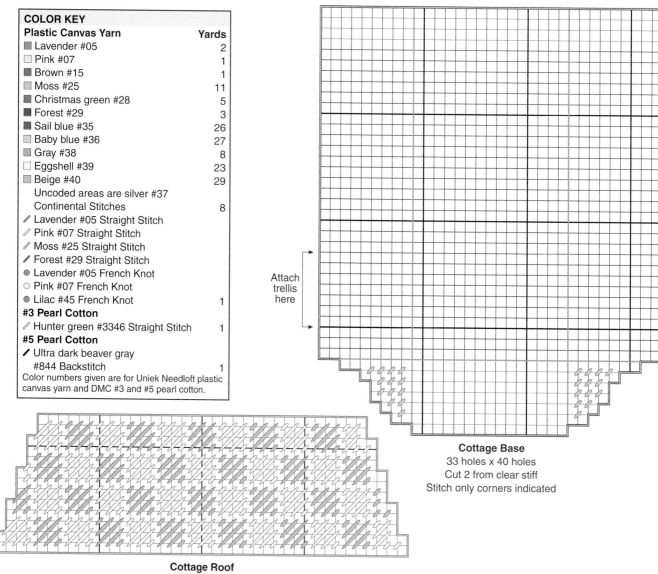

Cottage Base
33 holes x 40 holes
Cut 2 from clear stiff
Stitch only corners indicated

Attach trellis here

Cottage Roof
40 holes x 13 holes
Cut 4 from clear stiff

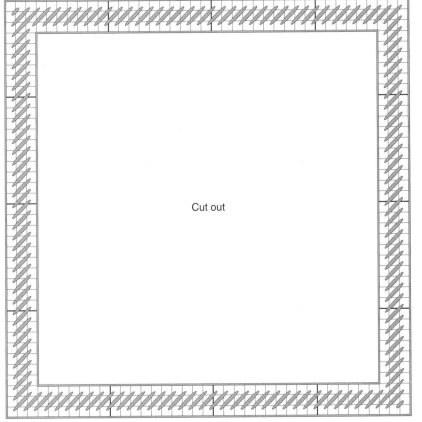

Cottage Overhang
39 holes x 39 holes
Cut 2 from clear stiff
Stitch as one

Cut out

Porch Side
7 holes x 6 holes
Cut 2, reverse 1, from clear stiff

Step Riser & Tread
15 holes x 3 holes
Cut 3 from clear stiff

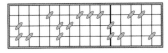

Porch Top
15 holes x 4 holes
Cut 1 from clear stiff

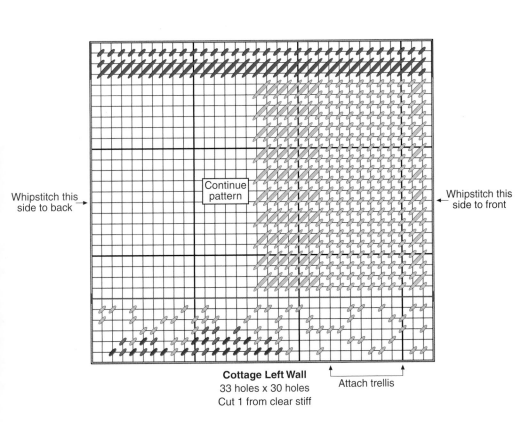

Whipstitch this side to back

Continue pattern

Whipstitch this side to front

Cottage Left Wall
33 holes x 30 holes
Cut 1 from clear stiff

Attach trellis

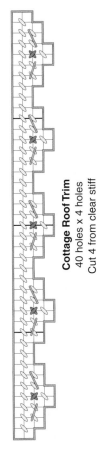

Cottage Roof Trim
40 holes x 4 holes
Cut 4 from clear stiff

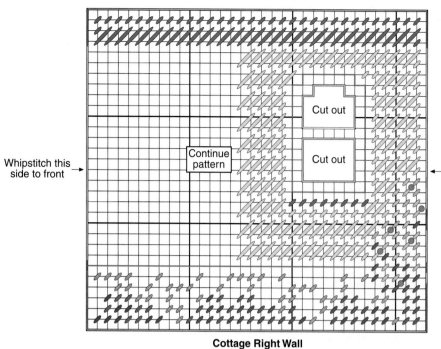

Whipstitch this side to front →

← Whipstitch this side to back

Continue pattern

Cut out

Cut out

Cottage Right Wall
33 holes x 30 holes
Cut 1 from clear stiff

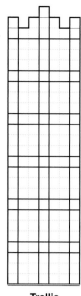

Trellis
7 holes x 26 holes
Cut 1 from almond,
cutting away blue lines
Do not stitch

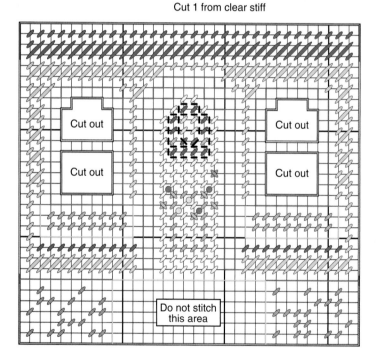

Cut out

Cut out

Cut out

Cut out

Do not stitch this area

Cottage Front Wall
33 holes x 30 holes
Cut 1 from clear stiff

Window Box Front
9 holes x 4 holes
Cut 2 from clear stiff

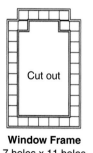

Cut out

Window Frame
7 holes x 11 holes
Cut 4 from clear stiff
Do not stitch

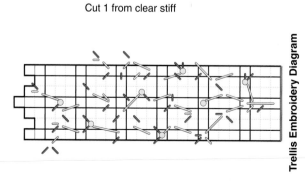

Trellis Embroidery Diagram

COLOR KEY	
Plastic Canvas Yarn	**Yards**
■ Lavender #05	2
□ Pink #07	1
■ Brown #15	1
▨ Moss #25	11
■ Christmas green #28	5
■ Forest #29	3
■ Sail blue #35	26
▨ Baby blue #36	27
▨ Gray #38	8
□ Eggshell #39	23
▨ Beige #40	29
Uncoded areas are silver #37	
Continental Stitches	8
⁄ Lavender #05 Straight Stitch	
⁄ Pink #07 Straight Stitch	
⁄ Moss #25 Straight Stitch	
⁄ Forest #29 Straight Stitch	
● Lavender #05 French Knot	
○ Pink #07 French Knot	
● Lilac #45 French Knot	1
#3 Pearl Cotton	
⁄ Hunter green #3346 Straight Stitch	1
#5 Pearl Cotton	
⁄ Ultra dark beaver gray #844 Backstitch	1
Color numbers given are for Uniek Needloft plastic canvas yarn and DMC #3 and #5 pearl cotton.	

Cottage Clip

Skill Level
Beginner

Size
4⅛ inches W x
3⅞ inches H x
1 inch D with clip

This decorative English cottage pulls double duty. It's decorative and also serves to keep snacks fresh in their bags!

Materials

- ¼ sheet 7-count plastic canvas
- Uniek Needloft plastic canvas yarn as listed in color key
- #8 pearl cotton as listed in color key
- #16 tapestry needle
- Mill Hill Products ceramic bow bunny #86043 from Gay Bowles Sales Inc.
- 3½-inch-wide junior-size bag clip with holes in handle
- Carpet thread
- Thick white glue

Instructions

1. Cut plastic canvas according to graph.

2. Stitch and Overcast cottage following graph, working uncoded areas with pink Continental Stitches.

3. Embroider flowers and leaves across front of roof with 1 ply yarn. Work black pearl cotton embroidery, leaving long vertical Straight Stitches unworked at this time.

4. Using a full strand yarn, Straight Stitch eggshell pickets of gate at center front, then work vertical black pearl cotton Straight Stitches immediately to the left of the eggshell Straight Stitches.

5. Using black pearl cotton, attach bunny button where indicated with blue dots.

6. Center bag clip behind cottage, making sure to keep bottom of clip slightly above bottom edge of stitched piece. Attach with carpet thread, working through holes at top of handle and around bar of front half at gate posts; add glue between clip and stitched piece just before completing. ✂

COLOR KEY

Plastic Canvas Yarn	Yards
▨ Lavender #05	1
☐ Moss #25	1
▨ Christmas green #28	1
■ Forest #29	1
☐ Baby blue #36	1
▨ Gray #38	1
☐ Eggshell #39	3
☐ Beige #40	4
Uncoded areas are pink #07 Continental Stitches	1
╱ Moss #25 Straight Stitch	
╱ Eggshell #39 Straight Stitch	
● Lavender #05 French Knot	
#8 Pearl Cotton	
╱ Black Backstitch and Straight Stitch	4

Color numbers given are for Uniek Needloft plastic canvas yarn.

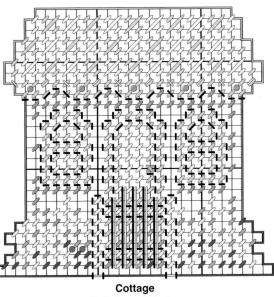

Cottage
27 holes x 25 holes
Cut 1

Design by
Janelle Giese

Floral Baskets

Skill Level
Beginner

Size
4¾ inches W x
5½ inches H x
4 inches D

You'll find dozens of uses for these pretty baskets! They're perfect for bridal showers, Mother's Day luncheons and just around the house!

Designs by
Kathleen Hurley

Materials
- 2 sheets 7-count plastic canvas
- Coats & Clark Red Heart Classic worsted weight yarn Art. E267 as listed in color key
- #16 tapestry needle
- Hot-glue gun

Instructions

1. Cut plastic canvas according to graphs (this page and pages 25 and 26), carefully cutting apart dogwood in corners indicated with arrows.

2. Stitch basket pieces following graphs, leaving both ends of each handle unworked.

3. For each basket, Whipstitch four sides together, then Whipstitch sides to one bottom; Overcast top edges. Overcast side edges of handle where indicated on graph, then glue unstitched portions of handle inside basket sides.

4. Stitch and Overcast flowers and leaves, leaving portions of pansy top and daffodil bottom unstitched where indicated.

5. Work paddy green Straight Stitches on leaves and yellow French Knots on blue and dogwood flowers when background stitching is completed.

6. Using photo as a guide through step 8, glue pansy back behind pansy front, covering unstitched portion of back.

7. Covering unstitched portion of bottom layer, glue daffodil top petals to daffodil bottom petals, placing top petals between bottom petals.

8. Glue one flower and one leaf to one side of each basket. ✄

COLOR KEY	
Worsted Weight Yarn	**Yards**
☐ White #1	66
■ Black #12	1
☐ Yellow #230	6
■ Orange #245	1
☐ Maize #261	2
☐ Light lavender #579	2
■ Purple #596	3
☐ Emerald green #676	1
■ Paddy green #686	6
■ Grenadine #730	2
☐ Pink #737	3
☐ Blue jewel #818	4
■ True blue #822	1
╱ Paddy green #686 Straight Stitch	
○ Yellow #230 French Knot	
Color numbers given are for Coats & Clark Red Heart Classic worsted weight yarn Art. E267.	

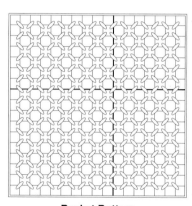

Basket Bottom
17 holes x 17 holes
Cut 4

Dogwood
21 holes x 21 holes
Cut 1

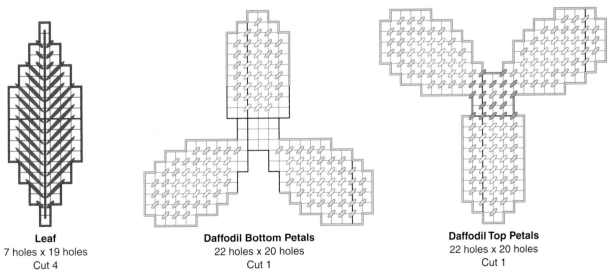

Leaf
7 holes x 19 holes
Cut 4

Daffodil Bottom Petals
22 holes x 20 holes
Cut 1

Daffodil Top Petals
22 holes x 20 holes
Cut 1

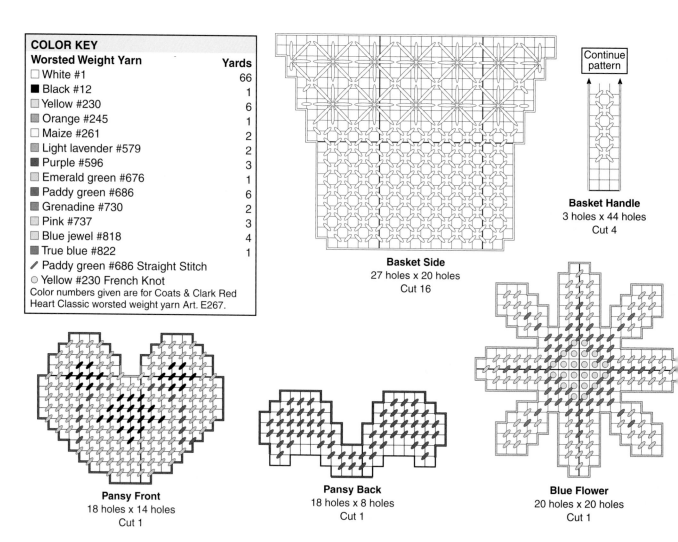

COLOR KEY

Worsted Weight Yarn	Yards
☐ White #1	66
■ Black #12	1
☐ Yellow #230	6
☐ Orange #245	1
☐ Maize #261	2
☐ Light lavender #579	2
■ Purple #596	3
☐ Emerald green #676	1
■ Paddy green #686	6
☐ Grenadine #730	2
☐ Pink #737	3
☐ Blue jewel #818	4
■ True blue #822	1
╱ Paddy green #686 Straight Stitch	
○ Yellow #230 French Knot	

Color numbers given are for Coats & Clark Red Heart Classic worsted weight yarn Art. E267.

Continue pattern

Basket Side
27 holes x 20 holes
Cut 16

Basket Handle
3 holes x 44 holes
Cut 4

Pansy Front
18 holes x 14 holes
Cut 1

Pansy Back
18 holes x 8 holes
Cut 1

Blue Flower
20 holes x 20 holes
Cut 1

Mini Trinket Boxes

Continued on page 13

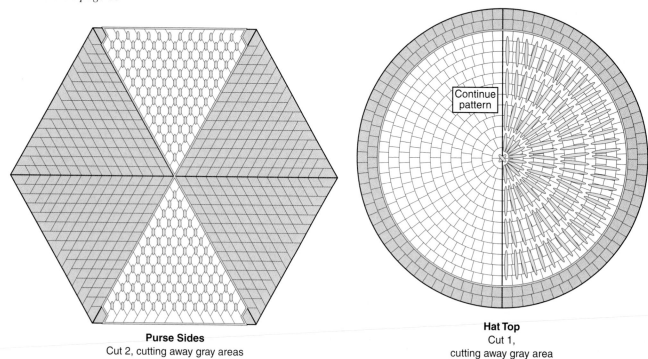

Continue pattern

Purse Sides
Cut 2, cutting away gray areas

Hat Top
Cut 1,
cutting away gray area

Nosy Bunny Tote

Materials

- 1½ sheets 7-count plastic canvas
- Coats & Clark Red Heart Super Saver worsted weight yarn Art. E300 and E301 as listed in color key
- #16 tapestry needle
- ½-inch white pompom
- 18 inches 20-gauge floral wire
- Hot-glue gun

Instructions

1. Cut plastic canvas according to graphs (page 28). Cut one 37-hole x 30-hole piece for tote back, one 37-hole x 15-hole piece for tote bottom and two 15-hole x 30-hole pieces for tote sides. Tote bottom will remain unstitched.

2. Continental Stitch back and sides with lavender. Stitch handle pieces, placing floral wire behind one piece before stitching then stitching

Skill Level
Beginner

Size
6½ inches W x
8¼ inches H x
2½ inches D

Tuck an Easter gift inside this cute little tote! It's just the right size for holding a big chocolate bunny!

Design by
Susan D. Fisher

over plastic canvas and wire.

3. Stitch front following graph, working uncoded background with lavender Continental Stitches.

4. When background stitching is completed, work lettering on tote front and all embroidery on handle pieces.

5. Stitch and Overcast feet, leaving intersections marked with a blue triangle unworked at this time.

6. Overcast top edges of front, back and sides with adjacent colors. Using lavender, Whipstitch front and back to sides,

then Whip-stitch front, back and sides to unstitched bottom.

7. Place feet on front (see photo); using petal pink, work stitches through both thicknesses over unstitched intersections in direction of previously worked stitches on feet.

8. Whipstitch wrong sides of handle pieces together. Tack eggs on end of handle to tote sides.

9. Glue pompom to tote front where indicated on graph with blue dot. ✂

COLOR KEY	
Worsted Weight Yarn	**Yards**
☐ White #311	2
☐ Pale yellow #322	4
▨ Buff #334	6
▨ Light periwinkle #347	4
☐ Petal pink #373	8
▨ Emerald green #676	4
Uncoded areas are lavender #358 Continental Stitches	53
╱ Lavender #358 Overcasting and Whipstitching	
╱ Petal pink #373 Backstitch and Straight Stitch	
╱ Grass green #687 Backstitch	2
○ Petal pink #373 French Knot	
● Raspberry #375 French Knot	2
Color numbers given are for Coats & Clark Red Heart Super Saver worsted weight yarn Art. E300 and Art. E301.	

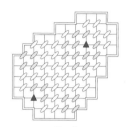

Foot
10 holes x 10 holes
Cut 2

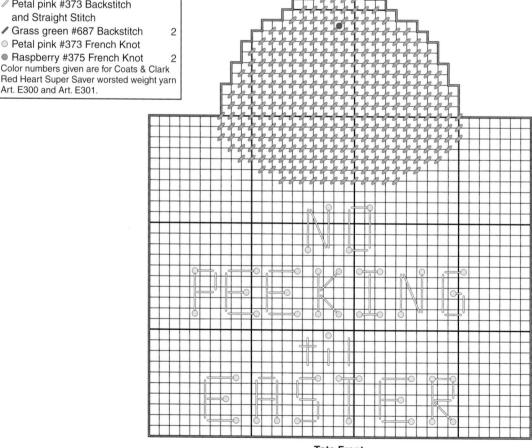

Tote Front
37 holes x 42 holes
Cut 1

Handle
7 holes x 79 holes
Cut 2

Bunny Ornament

Materials

- 1 Uniek QuickShape plastic canvas heart
- Uniek Needloft plastic canvas yarn as listed in color key
- #16 tapestry needle
- 8 inches ⅛-inch-wide yellow satin ribbon
- 7 inches fine gold cord
- Fabric glue

Instructions

1. Cut ornament from plastic canvas heart according to graph, cutting away gray areas.

2. Stitch and Overcast ornament following graph, stitching lilac, yellow and mermaid Straight Stitches while working background stitches.

3. When background stitching is completed, work Backstitches for mouth and French Knots for eyes with 1 ply black.

4. Tie yellow satin ribbon in a bow and glue to base of ears; trim ends.

5. Glue ends of fine gold cord behind years to form hanger. ✄

Skill Level
Beginner

Size
2¼ inches W x
5 inches H

Add a touch of Easter to cheer your home, office or car with this friendly bunny-in-an-egg ornament!

Design by
Joan Green

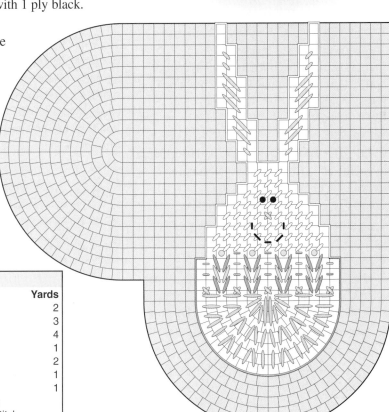

COLOR KEY

Plastic Canvas Yarn	Yards
☐ Pink #07	2
☐ Baby blue #36	3
☐ White #41	4
▨ Lilac #45	1
▨ Mermaid #53	2
☐ Yellow #57	1
✒ Black #00 Backstitch	1
⁄ Lilac #45 Straight Stitch	
⁄ Mermaid #53 Straight Stitch	
⁄ Yellow #57 Straight Stitch	
● Black #00 French Knot	
○ Pink #07 French Knot	

Color numbers given are for Uniek Needloft plastic canvas yarn.

Bunny Ornament
Cut 1,
cutting away gray areas

Pet Buddies

Skill Level
Beginner

Size
Designs vary in size from 3¼–3¾ inches W x 3¼–3¾inches H, excluding tails and legs.

Curly chenille stems add the finishing touch to this set of three whimsical animal magnets! Animal lovers will adore them!

Designs by Nancy Marshall

Materials
- ¾ sheet 7-count plastic canvas
- Uniek Needloft plastic canvas yarn as listed in color key
- 6-strand embroidery floss as listed in color key
- #16 tapestry needle
- Hand-sewing needle
- 6 (7mm) round black movable eyes
- 2 (6mm) round black beads
- 12-inch chenille stems: 5 yellow and 3 beige
- ¼-inch wooden dowel
- 3 button magnets or 2-inch adhesive-backed magnet strips
- Wire cutters
- Hot-glue gun

Bodies
1. Cut one of each animal from plastic canvas according to graphs.

2. Stitch and Overcast pieces following graphs, working uncoded areas on bluebird with bright blue Continental Stitches, uncoded areas on dog with sandstone Continental Stitches and uncoded areas on cat with yellow Continental Stitches.

3. When background stitching and Overcasting are completed, Backstitch mouths on dog and cat with black embroidery floss.

4. Using photo as a guide through step 5, for noses, sew round black beads to dog and cat with hand-sewing needle and 1 strand black floss.

5. Glue two eyes to each animal. Cut a 3-inch length of bright blue yarn and thread through top center hole of bird's head; knot and trim edges to about ½ inch, then fray edges of yarn with a needle.

Legs & Tails
1. For bird, cut a 9-inch length of yellow chenille stem. Leaving 1 inch at each end, wrap remainder around dowel; slide off.

2. For foot, cut a 2-inch length of yellow chenille stem and twist its center around one end of first coil (1 inch at end of coil becomes center "toe"). Insert other end of leg through body where indicated on graph and twist stem around itself to secure.

3. Repeat steps 1 and 2 to make a second leg.

4. For each leg of cat and dog, cut a 6-inch length of chenille stem, using yellow for cat and beige for dog. Leaving 1 inch at one end of stem, wrap remainder around dowel; slide off. Bend down last coil to form paw. Insert other end through body where indicated on graph and twist stem around itself to secure.

5. For tails, cut a 3-inch length of beige chenille stem for dog and a 4-inch length of yellow chenille stem for cat; secure one end through body where indicated on graphs and bend tails as shown.

6. Glue button magnets to wrong sides or cut self-adhesive strips to fit, then adhere to wrong sides of stitches pieces.

7. To finish as shelf sitters (as shown in photograph), do not glue magnets to back of animals. Instead, cut a piece of plastic canvas 6 holes by 10 holes; do not stitch. Glue top short edge of unstitched piece to back of animal to act as an easel to allow animals to sit upright. ✂

COLOR KEY	
Plastic Canvas Yarn	**Yards**
☐ White #41	2
☐ Yellow #57	6
▨ Bright orange #58	1
■ Bright blue #60	6
Uncoded areas on dog are sandstone #16 Continental Stitches	6
Uncoded areas on cat are yellow #57 Continental Stitches	
Uncoded areas on bird are bright blue #60 Continental Stitches	
⁄ Sandstone #16 Overcasting	
6-Strand Embroidery Floss	
⁄ Black Backstitch	1
● Attach leg	
● Attach tail	
Color numbers given are for Uniek Needloft plastic canvas yarn.	

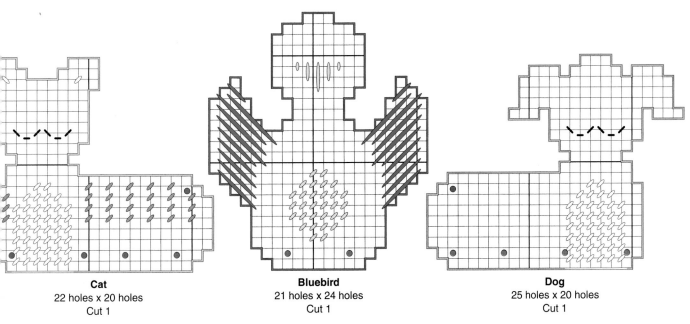

Cat
22 holes x 20 holes
Cut 1

Bluebird
21 holes x 24 holes
Cut 1

Dog
25 holes x 20 holes
Cut 1

Spring Calendar

Skill Level
Beginner

Size
11¼ inches W x
4⅛ inches H x
1⅞ inches D

Keep track of your months and days from March through May with this cheerful springtime calendar!

Materials
- 1 sheet 7-count plastic canvas
- Uniek Needloft plastic canvas yarn as listed in color key
- #16 tapestry needle
- Hot-glue gun

Project Note
Some graphs are shared with similar calendars in the other chapters of this book. Colors used for each season are given with the graphs and/or the instructions for that season.

Instructions
1. Cut plastic canvas according to graphs (this page and pages 33 and 34).

2. Cut one 17-hole x 9-hole piece for month block side and two 9-hole x 9-hole pieces for month block ends; stitch all three pieces with bright blue Continental Stitches.

3. Stitch and Overcast fence, bunnies, flowers and leaves, working uncoded areas on bunnies with camel Continental Stitches. Stitch remaining pieces, working uncoded areas on block pieces with bright blue Continental Stitches. Uncoded area on box back should remain unstitched.

4. Work French Knots on bunnies when background stitching is completed. Overcast one long edge of each box side.

5. Using bright blue through step 7, Whipstitch box back to remaining long edges of box sides, then Whipstitch box long sides to box short sides.

6. Whipstitch the four month block sides together along long edges, then Whipstitch month block ends to sides.

7. For each day block, Whipstitch six pieces together, making sure there is one each of numbers "0", "1" and "2" with each block.

8. Making sure bottom edges are even, center and glue box back to fence, and bunnies to fence on each side of box. Glue flowers and leaves to fence above box. Place month and day blocks in box. ✂

Calendar Flower
7 holes x 7 holes

COLOR KEY

Plastic Canvas Yarn	Yards
■ Fern #23	2
□ White #41	25
■ Watermelon #55	4
□ Yellow #57	1
■ Bright blue #60	44
Uncoded areas on bunnies are camel #43 Continental Stitches	6
Uncoded areas on block pieces are bright blue #60 Continental Stitches	
╱ Camel #43 Overcasting	
● Black #00 French Knot	1
● Watermelon #55 French Knot	
Color numbers given are for Uniek Needloft plastic canvas yarn.	

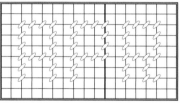

April Month Block Side
17 holes x 9 holes
Cut 1

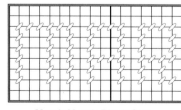

March Month Block Side
17 holes x 9 holes
Cut 1

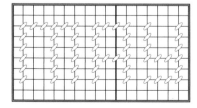

May Month Block Side
17 holes x 9 holes
Cut 1

Calendar Leaf
4 holes x 4 holes
Cut 6 for spring
Stitch as graphed
Cut 4 for summer
Stitch with holly

Design by
Angie Arickx

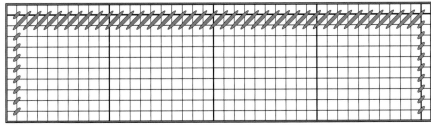

Box Back
41 holes x 11 holes
Cut 1 for each season
Stitch as graphed for spring
Stitch with fern for summer
Stitch with gold for autumn
Stitch with red for winter
Do not stitch uncoded area

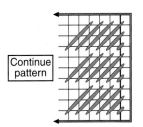

Continue
pattern

Box Long Side
41 holes x 10 holes
Cut 2 for each season
Stitch as graphed for spring
Stitch with fern for summer
Stitch with gold for autumn
Stitch with red for winter

Spring Fling **33**

COLOR KEY

Plastic Canvas Yarn	Yards
▢ Fern #23	2
▢ White #41	25
▢ Watermelon #55	4
▢ Yellow #57	1
▢ Bright blue #60	44
Uncoded areas on bunnies are camel #43 Continental Stitches	6
Uncoded areas on block pieces are bright blue #60 Continental Stitches	
⁄ Camel #43 Overcasting	
● Black #00 French Knot	1
● Watermelon #55 French Knot	

Color numbers given are for Uniek Needloft plastic canvas yarn.

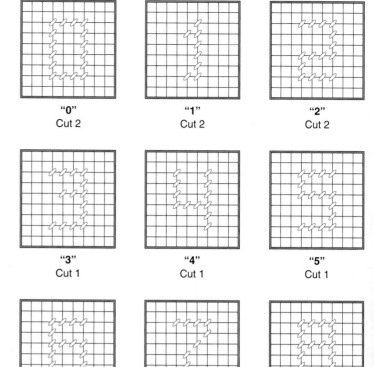

"0" Cut 2 **"1"** Cut 2 **"2"** Cut 2

"3" Cut 1 **"4"** Cut 1 **"5"** Cut 1

"6" and "9" Cut 1 **"7"** Cut 1 **"8"** Cut 1

Day Blocks
9 holes x 9 holes
Cut 1 set for each season
Stitch as graphed for spring
Stitch for summer, replacing bright blue with fern
Stitch for autumn, replacing bright blue with gold
Stitch for winter, replacing bright blue with red

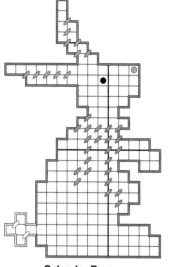

Calendar Bunny
15 holes x 24 holes
Cut 2, reverse 1

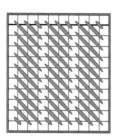

Box Short Side
10 holes x 11 holes
Cut 2 for each season
Stitch as graphed for spring
Stitch with fern for summer
Stitch with gold for autumn
Stitch with red for winter

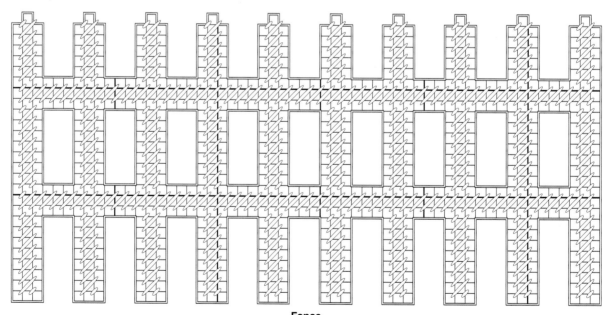

Fence
57 holes x 27 holes
Cut 1 for each season
Stitch as graphed for spring and summer
Stitch with eggshell for autumn
Stitch with camel for winter

Birds of Beauty

Skill Level
Beginner

Size
4⅜ inches W x
3⅛ inches H,
excluding poke

If you have occasion to give a friend a lush green plant, add an extra-special touch by including one of these pretty plant pokes.

Instructions

1. Cut plastic canvas according to graphs (page 40). Cut felt slightly smaller all around than birds.

2. Stitch and Overcast birds following graphs, working one bird as graphed. Work remaining bird replacing pearl cotton as follows: medium blue with light yellow and light yellow with coral. Replace royal blue metallic yarn with copper metallic yarn.

3. Stitch and Overcast wings following graphs, working French Knots last. Work one wing as graphed; work remaining wing replacing pearl cotton as follows: light blue with dark yellow and light yellow with coral. Replace royal blue metallic yarn with copper metallic yarn.

4. Using photo as a guide through step 6, glue corresponding wings to each bird with fabric glue.

5. For tails, curve each length of 20-gauge wire. Using jewel glue, coat end of wire and slip bead onto end. Allow to dry thoroughly.

6. For pokes, loosely coil 18-inch lengths 16-gauge wire. Using jewel glue throughout, center and glue one behind each bird. Glue two tail lengths to wrong side of each bird's tail. Allow to dry thoroughly.

7. Apply corresponding color of felt to back of birds. ✂

Graphs continued on page 40

Materials

- ⅓ sheet 10-count plastic canvas
- Coats & Clark Anchor #3 pearl cotton as listed in color key
- ¹⁄₁₆ inch-wide Plastic Canvas 10 Metallic Needlepoint Yarn by Rainbow Gallery as listed in color key
- #18 tapestry needle
- 3½-inch x 2½-inch piece each royal blue and gold self-adhesive Presto felt from Kunin Felt
- 4 (10mm) decorative gold or copper beads
- 4 (4-inch) lengths 20-gauge gold wire
- 2 (18-inch) lengths 16-gauge gold wire
- Fabric glue
- Jewel glue

Design by
Joan Green

Fairy Ornaments

Skill Level
Intermediate

Size
Bee Parade: 4¼ inches W x 6 inches H, excluding bees

Moth Flight: 4¼ inches W x 5¾ inches H

Peaceful Forest: 4⅝ inches W x 4¾ inches H

Add a touch of elfin magic to your spring with this set of three darling ornaments!

Designs by Janelle Giese

Materials
- 1 sheet clear stiff 7-count plastic canvas
- Small amount black 7-count plastic canvas
- Coats & Clark Red Heart Classic worsted weight yarn Art. E267 as listed in color key
- Coats & Clark Red Heart Super Saver worsted weight yarn Art. E300 as listed in color key
- Kreinik Heavy (#32) Braid as listed in color key
- DMC #5 pearl cotton as listed in color key
- DMC #8 pearl cotton as listed in color key
- #16 tapestry needle
- 21 inches fine white braid or cord
- 8 inches 30-gauge white covered stem wire
- Small dowel
- Thick white glue

Project Notes
Work first stitch of heavy (#32) braid Cross Stitches on wings and toadstool from lower right to upper left. Work the Cross Stitch from lower left to upper right, noting that some top stitches are a different color than the bottom stitch. Cross Stitches on toadstool are worked over Continental Stitches.

For all remaining Cross Stitches, work first stitch with yarn from lower left to upper right; work Cross Stitch with heavy (#32) braid from lower right to upper left.

Cutting & Stitching
1. Cut bees from black plastic canvas; cut remaining pieces from clear stiff plastic canvas according to graphs (pages 37 and 41).

2. Continental Stitch bees with black following graph, then Straight Stitch honey gold stripes. Backstitch wings with pearl braid, passing over two times; do not cut braid.

3. Place one bee near center of wire, then use braid to Whipstitch bee to wire; cut braid and apply dab of glue to secure. Repeat for remaining bee, spacing them about 1 inch apart. Curl wire around small dowel. Set aside.

4. Continental Stitch, Cross Stitch (see Project Notes) and Overcast remaining pieces following graphs, working uncoded areas with light clay Continental Stitches.

5. Using a full strand yarn, work light periwinkle French Knots on peaceful forest; use black to work Backstitches around spot on moth and Straight Stitch for "hanger" on lantern. Use two plies white yarn to work Straight Stitches and French Knots on moth.

6. Work pearl braid Cross Stitches on toadstool. On moth flight, work light peach braid Straight Stitches for lantern glow, passing over flame two times. Work cheeks on all fairies with dark salmon #8 pearl cotton.

7. With the exception of eye highlights (Pin Stitch), use black #5 pearl cotton to work all remaining embroidery, passing over eye on bee parade four times, eye on moth flight three times, and eyes on peaceful forest two times. Use two strands black pearl cotton on moth flight where indicated.

8. For Pin Stitches on eyes, bring pearl braid up in hole indicated above stitch, go down through black pearl cotton, splitting stitch, then back through same hole in which stitch originated.

Finishing
1. For moth antennae, attach a full strand of nickel to back of moth's head at bottom left, allowing one end to extend at front of head. Separate plies and trim.

2. Whipstitch end of bee wire to back of white flower at top of bee parade. Arrange as desired, then clip wire ends. Apply dab of glue to wire on backside of flower to secure.

3. Cut fine white braid or cord into three 7-inch lengths. Thread ends from front to back through holes indicated with red dots on graphs. Knot ends on backside so loop extends 3 inches above top of stitched piece; trim ends as needed. To secure, glue knot to backside. ✄

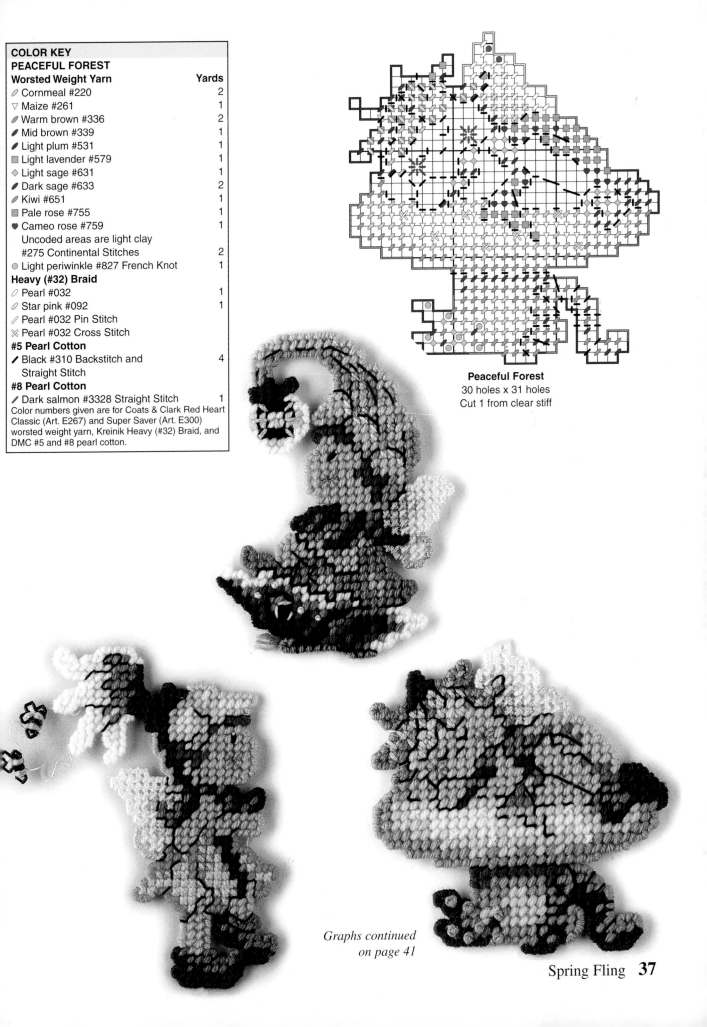

Peaceful Forest
30 holes x 31 holes
Cut 1 from clear stiff

Graphs continued on page 41

Spring Fling **37**

Spring Chicks Basket

Skill Level
Beginner

Size
3⅞ inches H x 6⅞ inches in diameter

Fill this sweet basket with your family's favorite Easter goodies, from jelly beans to marshmallow bunnies!

Materials
- 2 sheets 7-count plastic canvas
- Coats & Clark Red Heart Classic worsted weight yarn Art. E267 as listed in color key
- #16 tapestry needle

Instructions

1. Cut plastic canvas according to graphs (this page and page 40).

2. Stitch pieces following graphs, working uncoded area on side pieces with blue jewel Continental Stitches and placing three holes on right end of each side piece behind three holes on left end of other side piece before stitching, forming a circle.

3. When background stitching is completed, use 2 plies brown to Backstitch around chicks and work French Knot eyes. Use 2 plies to work forest green Straight Stitches. Work French Knots for flowers with 4 plies pink and lavender.

4. Using paddy green, Whipstitch basket bottom to basket side, easing around curves as needed. ✂

COLOR KEY	
Worsted Weight Yarn	**Yards**
▣ Orange #245	2
☐ Maize #261	16
▨ Paddy green #686	26
Uncoded areas are blue jewel #818 Continental Stitches	24
╱ Blue jewel #818 Overcasting	
╱ Mid brown #339 (2-ply) Backstitch	5
╱ Forest green #689 (2-ply) Straight Stitch	1
● Mid brown #339 (2-ply) French Knot	
● Lavender #584 (2-ply) French Knot	2
○ Pink #737 (4-ply) French Knot	2
Color numbers given are for Coats & Clark Red Heart Classic worsted weight yarn Art. E267.	

Design by Kathleen Hurley

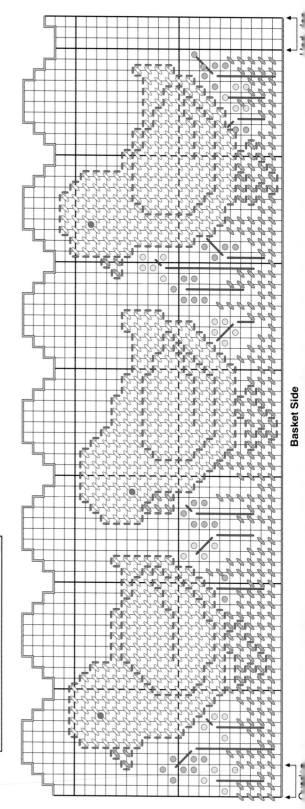

Basket Side

COLOR KEY

Worsted Weight Yarn	Yards
■ Orange #245	2
□ Maize #261	16
▨ Paddy green #686	26
Uncoded areas are blue jewel #818 Continental Stitches	24
⁄ Blue jewel #818 Overcasting	
⁄ Mid brown #339 (2-ply) Backstitch	5
⁄ Forest green #689 (2-ply) Straight Stitch	1
● Mid brown #339 (2-ply) French Knot	
● Lavender #584 (2-ply) French Knot	2
○ Pink #737 (4-ply) French Knot	2

Color numbers given are for Coats & Clark Red Heart Classic worsted weight yarn Art. E267.

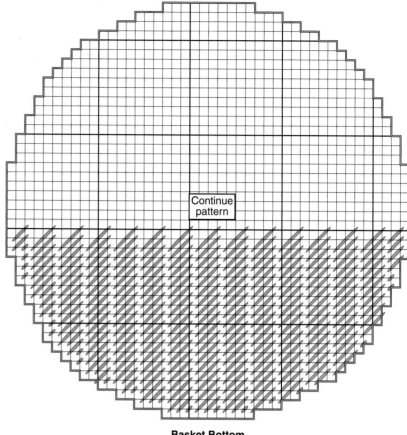

Continue pattern

Basket Bottom
44 holes x 44 holes
Cut 1

Birds of Beauty

Continued from page 35

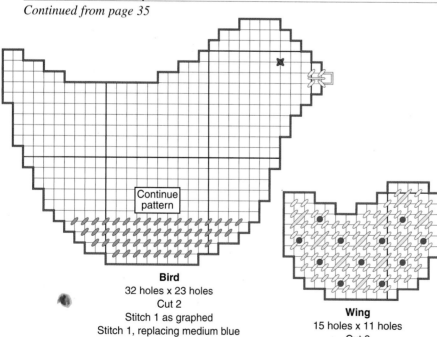

Continue pattern

Bird
32 holes x 23 holes
Cut 2
Stitch 1 as graphed
Stitch 1, replacing medium blue
with light yellow, light yellow with
coral, and royal blue with copper

Wing
15 holes x 11 holes
Cut 2
Stitch 1 as graphed
Stitch 1, replacing light blue
with dark yellow, light yellow with
coral, and royal blue with copper

COLOR KEY

#3 Pearl Cotton	Yards
□ Light blue #144	1
■ Medium blue #146	6
□ Light yellow #301	7
Dark yellow #302	1
Coral #328	1
⁄ Light yellow #301 Straight Stitch	
1/16-Inch Metallic Needlepoint Yarn	
Copper #PM53	4
■ Royal blue #PM56	4
● Royal blue #PM56 French Knot	

Color numbers given are for Coats & Clark Anchor #3 pearl cotton and Rainbow Gallery Plastic Canvas 10 Metallic Needlepoint Yarn.

Fairy Ornaments

Continued from page 37

COLOR KEY
MOTH FLIGHT

Worsted Weight Yarn	Yards
⟋ Off-white #03	2
◆ Black #12	1
⟋ Cornmeal #220	1
⟋ Medium coral #252	1
♥ Mid brown #339	1
▲ Coffee #365	1
⟋ Nickel #401	2
⟋ Light plum $531	1
▽ Light lavender #579	1
◇ Light sage #631	1
⟋ Dark sage #633	1
⟋ Blue jewel #818	2
⟋ Light periwinkle #827	1
Uncoded areas are light clay #275 Continental Stitches	2
⟋ Light clay #275 Overcasting	
⟋ Off-white #3 Staight Stitch	
⟋ Black #12 Backstitch and Straight Stitch	
○ Off-white #3 French Knot	

Heavy (#32) Braid

⟋ Pearl #032	1
⟋ Star mauve #093	1
⟋ Light peach #9192 Straight Stitch	1
⟋ Pearl #032 Pin Stitch	

#5 Pearl Cotton

⟋ Black #310 (1- strand) Backstitch and Straight Stitch	4
⟋ Black #310 (2- strand) Backstitch and Straight Stitch	

#8 Pearl Cotton

⟋ Dark salmon #3328 Straight Stitch	1

Color numbers given are for Coats & Clark Red Heart Classic (Art. E267) and Super Saver (Art. E300) worsted weight yarn, Kreinik Heavy (#32) Braid, and DMC #5 and #8 pearl cotton.

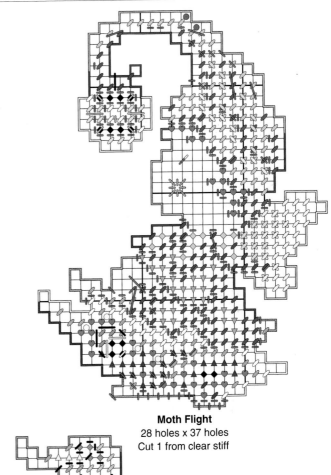

Moth Flight
28 holes x 37 holes
Cut 1 from clear stiff

Bee
3 holes x 4 holes
Cut 2 from black

Bee Parade
27 holes x 39 holes
Cut 1 from clear stiff

COLOR KEY
BEE PARADE

Worsted Weight Yarn	Yards
⟋ Off-white #03	2
⟋ Black #12	1
⟋ Cornmeal #220	1
⟋ Sea coral #246	1
⟋ Medium coral #252	2
△ Maize #261	1
● Bronze #286	1
⟋ Light sage #631	1
◆ Dark sage #633	2
◇ Kiwi #651	1
Uncoded areas are light clay #275 Continental Stitches	2
⟋ Light clay #275 Overcasting	
⟋ Honey gold #645 Straight Stitch	1

Heavy (#32) Braid

⟋ Pearl #032	1
⟋ Light peach #9192	2
⟋ Pearl #032 Backstitch and Pin Stitch	

#5 Pearl Cotton

⟋ Black #310 Backstitch and Straight Stitch	3

#8 Pearl Cotton

⟋ Dark salmon #3328 Straight Stitch	1

Color numbers given are for Coats & Clark Red Heart Classic (Art. E267) and Super Saver (Art. E300) worsted weight yarn, Kreinik Heavy (#32) Braid, and DMC #5 and #8 pearl cotton.

Birdies Welcome

Skill Level

Beginner

Size

Sign: 10¾ inches W x 19¼ inches H

Coaster: 3¼ inches W x 4⅜ inches H

Holder: 3⅜ inches W x 3¼ inches H x 2¾ inches D

Whether you are a snowbird, or you just like birds and birdhouses, this vibrant welcome sign and matching coaster set will make sweet additions to your home!

Designs by Janelle Giese

Materials

- 2 sheets artist-size 7-count plastic canvas
- 1 regular-size sheet clear 7-count plastic canvas
- 1 sheet white 7-count plastic canvas
- Uniek Needloft plastic canvas yarn as listed in color key
- #5 pearl cotton as listed in color key
- #8 pearl cotton as listed in color key
- #16 tapestry needle
- Saw-tooth hanger
- Carpet thread

Instructions

1. Match pink lines of two welcome sign graphs, then cut as one piece from artist-size plastic canvas according to graphs (pages 44 and 45), cutting two 71-hole x 128-hole pieces.

2. Cut six coasters, one holder front, one holder back and two holder sides from clear plastic canvas; cut six coasters and one holder base from white plastic canvas according to graphs (pages 44 and 45). Do not stitch coasters cut from white plastic canvas.

3. Matching edges, place sign pieces together, then stitch and Overcast as one following graphs, working uncoded areas with white Continental Stitches. Work two stitches per hole with black yarn where indicated for openings on birdhouses

4. Stitch and Overcast feet on holder base, leaving remaining area indicated unstitched. Stitch remaining pieces working uncoded areas with white Continental Stitches. Work two stitches per hole with black yarn where indicated for openings on birdhouses.

5. When background stitching is completed, work embroidery, using a full strand royal yarn to Straight Stitch feathers at top of birdies' heads. Use 1 ply yarn to work Lazy Daisy Stitches on birdhouse gables and Straight Stitches for flowers on sign.

6. Work remaining embroidery with pearl cotton following graphs, wrapping white pearl cotton two times around needle for French Knots, and working two stitches per hole where indicated for beak on holder front.

7. Whipstitch holder sides to holder front and back, then Whipstitch front, back and sides to base, placing feet in front. Overcast remaining edges.

8. Place one unstitched white coaster behind each stitched coaster, then Whipstitch together following graph. Place coasters in holder.

9. Using carpet thread, center and sew saw-tooth hanger to backside of top gable on sign. ✂

Back of coaster holder

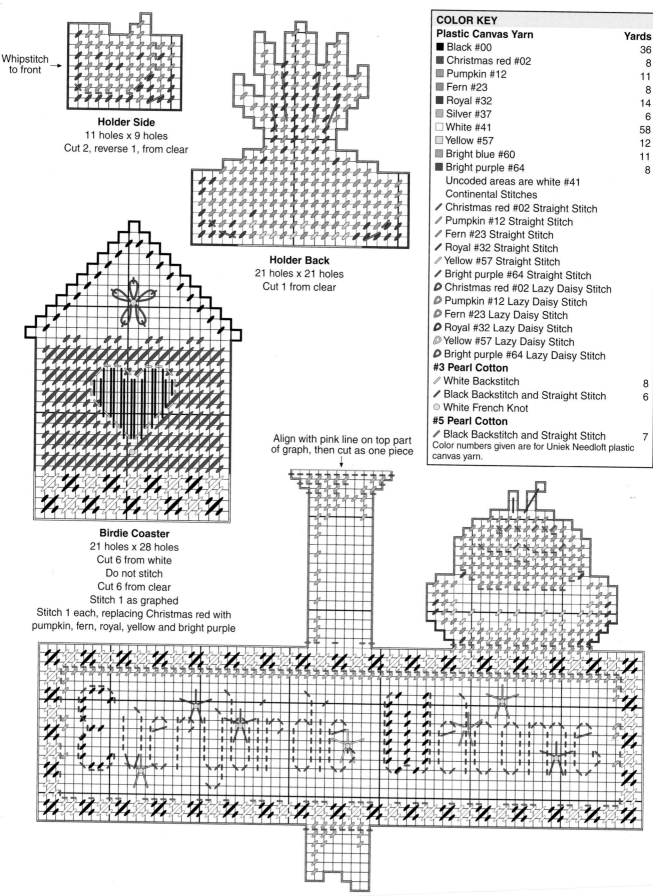

Whipstitch to front →

Holder Side
11 holes x 9 holes
Cut 2, reverse 1, from clear

Holder Back
21 holes x 21 holes
Cut 1 from clear

COLOR KEY

Plastic Canvas Yarn — Yards

■	Black #00	36
■	Christmas red #02	8
■	Pumpkin #12	11
■	Fern #23	8
■	Royal #32	14
■	Silver #37	6
□	White #41	58
□	Yellow #57	12
■	Bright blue #60	11
■	Bright purple #64	8

Uncoded areas are white #41
Continental Stitches
✦ Christmas red #02 Straight Stitch
✦ Pumpkin #12 Straight Stitch
✦ Fern #23 Straight Stitch
✦ Royal #32 Straight Stitch
✦ Yellow #57 Straight Stitch
✦ Bright purple #64 Straight Stitch
Ɒ Christmas red #02 Lazy Daisy Stitch
Ɒ Pumpkin #12 Lazy Daisy Stitch
Ɒ Fern #23 Lazy Daisy Stitch
Ɒ Royal #32 Lazy Daisy Stitch
Ɒ Yellow #57 Lazy Daisy Stitch
Ɒ Bright purple #64 Lazy Daisy Stitch

#3 Pearl Cotton
✦ White Backstitch — 8
✦ Black Backstitch and Straight Stitch — 6
○ White French Knot

#5 Pearl Cotton
✦ Black Backstitch and Straight Stitch — 7
Color numbers given are for Uniek Needloft plastic canvas yarn.

Birdie Coaster
21 holes x 28 holes
Cut 6 from white
Do not stitch
Cut 6 from clear
Stitch 1 as graphed
Stitch 1 each, replacing Christmas red with
pumpkin, fern, royal, yellow and bright purple

Align with pink line on top part
of graph, then cut as one piece

Welcome Sign
71 holes x 128 holes
Cut 2 from artist-size sheets

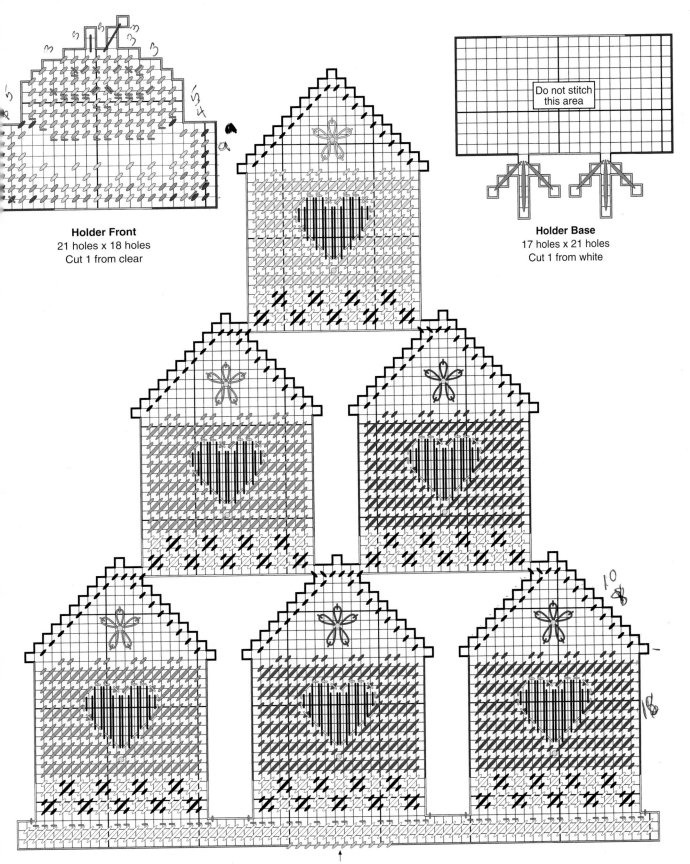

Holder Front
21 holes x 18 holes
Cut 1 from clear

Holder Base
17 holes x 21 holes
Cut 1 from white

Do not stitch
this area

Welcome Sign
Align with pink line on bottom
part of graph and cut as one
from artist-size plastic canvas,
cutting two 71-hole x 128-hole pieces

Funky Chicken Tissue Topper

Skill Level
Beginner

Size
Fits boutique-style tissue box

Go wild when you choose colors to stitch this zany chicken tissue box cover!

Design by
Michele Wilcox

Materials
- 1½ sheets 7-count plastic canvas
- Uniek Needloft plastic canvas yarn as listed in color key
- #3 pearl cotton as listed in color key
- #16 tapestry needle
- Hot-glue gun

Instructions
1. Cut plastic canvas according to graphs.

2. Stitch and Overcast chicken following graph, working uncoded area with turquoise Continental Stitches.

3. When background stitching is completed, work French Knot eye with black pearl cotton.

4. Stitch topper pieces following graphs. Overcast inside edges on top, and bottom edges on sides. Whipstitch sides together, then Whipstitch sides to top.

5. Center and glue chicken to one side, making sure bottom edges are even. ✂

COLOR KEY

Plastic Canvas Yarn	Yards
▨ Moss #25	100
▨ Watermelon #55	2
☐ Yellow #57	1
▨ Bright purple #57	1
Uncoded area is turquoise #54 Continental Stitches	15
⁄ Turquoise #54 Overcasting	
#3 Pearl Cotton	
● Black French Knot	1

Color numbers given are for Uniek Needloft plastic canvas yarn.

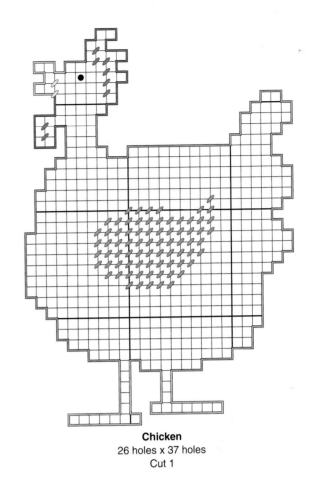

Chicken
26 holes x 37 holes
Cut 1

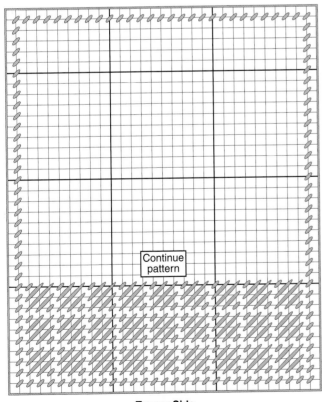

Topper Side
30 holes x 36 holes
Cut 4

Continue pattern

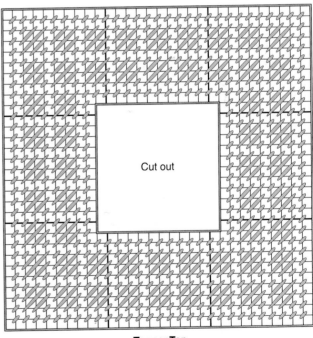

Cut out

Topper Top
30 holes x 30 holes
Cut 1

Flower Frames Screen

Skill Level
Beginner

Size
One Frame: 5 inches W x 6½ inches H
Screen: 25½ inches W x 6½ inches H

Display your favorite springtime memories in these floral frames stitched in a garden of colors!

Design by Nancy Marshall

Materials
- 2½ sheets 7-count plastic canvas
- Uniek Needloft plastic canvas yarn as listed in color key
- #16 tapestry needle
- Mill Hill Products ceramic bumble bee button #86128 and ceramic ladybug button #86050 from Gay Bowles Sales Inc
- Hand-sewing needle
- Sewing thread to match buttons
- Transparent thread

Instructions
1. Cut five each of frame fronts and frame backs from plastic canvas according to graph, cutting out center hole on frame fronts only. Backs will remain unstitched.

2. Stitch fronts following graphs, working one frame as graphed and one each replacing yellow with pink, watermelon, bright blue and bright purple. On frames with watermelon and bright purple flowers, replace holly with fern. When stitching leaves, work two stitches per holes as necessary to cover canvas.

3. Using adjacent colors, Overcast top edges of frame fronts from dot to dot.

4. Using sewing needle and matching thread, sew bumble bee button to watermelon frame where indicated on graph; sew ladybug button to bright purple frame where indicated on graph.

5. Using adjacent colors, Whipstitch one back to each front around side and bottom edges from dot to dot.

6. Placing frames with fern leaves between frames with holly leaves, sew frames together between brackets with transparent thread; knot thread securely. ✄

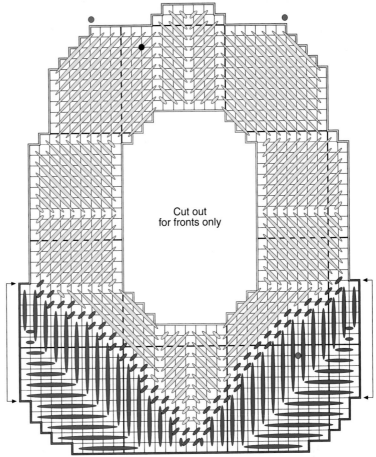

Cut out
for fronts only

COLOR KEY

Plastic Canvas Yarn	Yards
Pink #07	12
Fern #23	14
■ Holly #27	14
Watermelon #55	12
☐ Yellow #57	12
Bright blue #60	12
Bright purple #64	12
● Attach bumble bee button	
● Attach ladybug button	

Color numbers given are for Uniek Needloft plastic canvas yarn.

Flower Frame Front & Back
33 holes x 42 holes
Cut 5 for fronts
Stitch 1 as graphed
Stitch 1 each, replacing yellow with pink,
watermelon, bright blue and bright purple
Stitch leaves on watermelon and bright purple
flower frames, replacing holly with fern
Cut 5 for backs
Do not stitch

Wind Chime Birdhouse

Designs by
Joan Green

Skill Level

Beginner

Size

6⅜ inches W x
9¼ inches H x 3¼
inches D, including
chimes

Hung

from your

favorite

sunny win-

dow, this

cheerful

birdhouse

will bring

you tinkling

music when

you open

the window

to catch

a spring

breeze!

Materials

- ½ sheet 7-count plastic canvas
- 2 Uniek QuickShape plastic canvas stars
- Uniek Needloft plastic canvas yarn as listed in color key
- #16 tapestry needle
- 5 goldtone wind chimes
- 1¼-inch mushroom bird
- 24 inches fine gold thread
- Sewing needle
- 5 (4-inch) lengths 24-gauge gold #15036V Fun Wire from Amaco
- Gold self-adhesive Presto felt from Kunin Felt
- Fabric glue

Cutting & Stitching

1. Cut plastic canvas according to graphs, cutting away gray area in center of one star shape (birdhouse front). Do not cut second star shape (birdhouse back) which will remain unstitched.

2. Cut gold felt to fit birdhouse back; set aside.

3. Following graphs throughout stitching and assembly, stitch birdhouse front, Overcasting opening while stitching.

4. Stitch remaining pieces, working uncoded areas on roof sections with yellow Continental Stitches.

5. When background stitching is completed, work Backstitches for leaves and French Knots for flowers on roof sections.

Assembly

1. Overcast front and back along top edges from dot to dot. Whipstitch six side and bottom pieces together along long edges, forming one long strip, then Whipstitch around side and bottom edges of front and back from dot to dot. Overcast top edges of sides.

2. Whipstitch top edges of roof small sections together, then Whipstitch top edges of roof large sections to bottom edges of roof small sections. Overcast remaining edges with Christmas green.

3. Thread a wind chime onto each 4-inch length of wire to center of wire. Fold wire up and twist around each other. Dab fabric glue on ends and push through holes at bottom of birdhouse at regular intervals, so that tops of chimes are even. Bend wire down on inside, then allow to dry thoroughly.

4. For hanger, fold fine gold thread in half and thread through sewing needle. Thread needle through center top of roof; tie ends in a tight knot; pull knot through to wrong side.

5. Center and glue roof to top of birdhouse. Adhere felt to back of birdhouse. Glue mushroom bird to roof as in photo. ✄

COLOR KEY	
Plastic Canvas Yarn	**Yards**
☐ Tangerine #11	18
☐ Baby yellow #21	7
☐ Moss #25	3
☐ Watermelon #55	5
☐ Yellow #57	26
Uncoded areas are yellow #57 Continental Stitches	
✎ Christmas green #28 Backstitch and Overcasting	6
● Watermelon #55 French Knot	
Color numbers given are for Uniek Needloft plastic canvas yarn.	

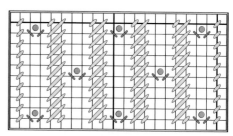

Birdhouse Roof Small Section
21 holes x 11 holes
Cut 2

Fruit Fairies

Skill Level

Intermediate

Size

5⅛ inches W x
5½ inches H

Bearing some of the season's favorite fruits, this charming trio of ornaments is sure to bring you happiness and good luck!

Designs by
Vicki Blizzard

Materials

- 3 sheets 7-count plastic canvas
- Coats & Clark Red Heart Classic worsted weight yarn Art. E267 as listed in color key
- #16 tapestry needle
- 12 inches each ⅛-inch-wide satin ribbon: yellow, white and deep pink
- Size 8 all-metal knitting needle
- Cookie sheet
- Casserole dish or heavy oven-proof object
- Clear monofilament thread or magnet strip
- Hot-glue gun

Cutting & Stitching

1. Cut plastic canvas according to graphs (page 60).

2. Work uncoded areas throughout all stitching with lily pink Continental Stitches unless otherwise instructed. Stitch and Overcast hands, hearts, and strawberry heart cap, reversing one hand in each pair of hands before stitching.

3. Overcast strawberry flower, working yellow French Knot with 2 plies yarn. Stitch all remaining pieces.

4. When background stitching is completed, use full strand yarn to work white Straight Stitches on lemon fairy wings and heart, paddy green Straight Stitches on strawberry wings, and pink Straight Stitches for noses on fairy front pieces, passing over each nose four times.

5. Work French Knots using 2 plies yarn.

6. Overcast around bottom edges of each fairy front and back between arrows.

Assembly

1. Whipstitch wrong sides of corresponding fronts and backs together along unworked edges. Whipstitch wrong sides of corresponding wings together so that each fairy has two sets of wings. Whipstitch wrong sides of legs together.

2. Run a bead of glue along top front and back edges of assembled legs and insert into bodies.

3. Using photo as a guide through step 5, glue strawberry heart, cap and flower together.

4. Making sure thumbs are up, glue wrist edges of hands to side edges of fairies between blue dots, Then glue ends of fingers to sides of corresponding hearts. Glue wings to backs of corresponding fairies.

5. Using white for lemon fairy, yellow for strawberry fairy and deep pink for watermelon fairy, tie ribbon in a bow around neck; trim ends diagonally.

Finishing

1. Preheat oven to 225 degrees. Cut paddy green, yellow and white yarn into five 1 yard lengths.

2. Working with single 1-yard lengths at a time, wrap yarn tightly around knitting needle. Place on cookie sheet and weight down with casserole dish or heavy oven-proof object to keep yarn from unwinding. Bake for 15 minutes.

Remove from oven and allow to cool completely before removing from knitting needle.

3. Use paddy green for watermelon fairy, yellow for strawberry fairy and white for lemon fairy. Following Figs. 1 and 2, apply glue to front top edge of head and press curl length into glue, working from center of length. Apply glue to sides and press curls into place.

4. Trim curls to desired length and glue to shoulders as needed (see photo).

5. Depending on length of hair desired, work with small amounts of glue and 1–3 inch lengths of curls to cover backs of heads (Fig. 3).

6. Finishing options: Hang with monofilament or glue magnet to backs. ✂

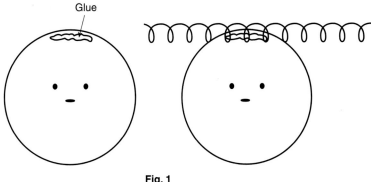

Fig. 1

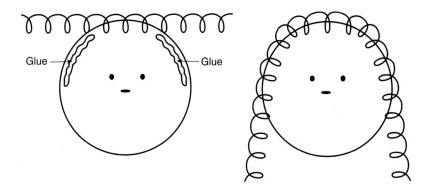

Fig. 2

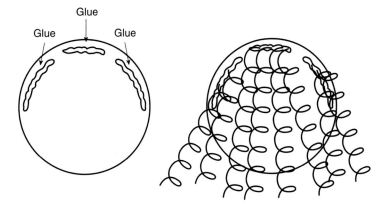

Fig. 3

Fairy Hand
7 holes x 5 holes
Cut 2, reverse 1, for each

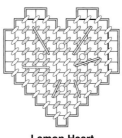

Lemon Heart
11 holes x 11 holes
Cut 1

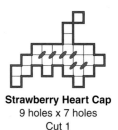

Strawberry Heart Cap
9 holes x 7 holes
Cut 1

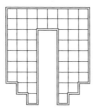

Fairy Legs
8 holes x 9 holes
Cut 2 for each

Strawberry Flower
3 holes x 3 holes
Cut 1

Lemon Fairy Wing
16 holes x 7 holes
Cut 4

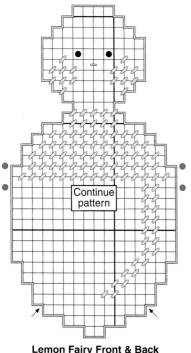

Lemon Fairy Front & Back
16 holes x 31 holes
Cut 2
Do not stitch facial features on back

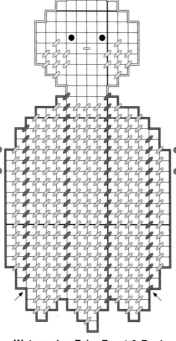

Watermelon Fairy Front & Back
16 holes x 32 holes
Cut 2
Do not stitch facial features on back

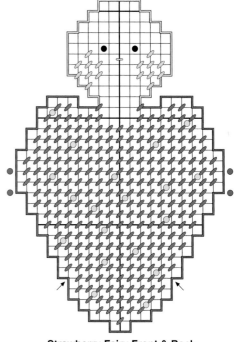

Strawberry Fairy Front & Back
20 holes x 31 holes
Cut 2
Do not stitch facial features on back

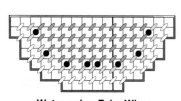

Watermelon Fairy Wing
16 holes x 7 holes
Cut 4

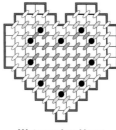

Watermelon Heart
11 holes x 11 holes
Cut 1

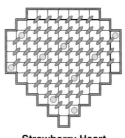

Strawberry Heart
11 holes x 11 holes
Cut 1

Strawberry Fairy Wing
13 holes x 16 holes
Cut 4

Summer Fling Wall Ornament

Materials

- 12 x 18-inch sheet 7-count plastic canvas
- Uniek Needloft plastic canvas yarn as listed in color key
- #3 pearl cotton as listed in color key
- #16 tapestry needle
- 1 yard ¼-inch-wide green satin ribbon

Instructions

1. Cut plastic canvas according to graph.

2. Stitch and Overcast piece following graph, working uncoded areas on frog with lemon Continental Stitches and uncoded area on bird with sail blue Continental Stitches.

3. When background stitching is completed, work pearl cotton embroidery as follows: black Straight Stitches and Backstitches on frog and ladybug; orange Straight Stitches on bird; blue French Knots on bee; and black French Knots on bird, ladybug and frog.

4. Double 1-yard length of green ribbon and attach through hole at top of ornament with a Lark's Head Knot. Tie ends of ribbon in a bow approximately 2 inches above knot. ✄ See photo on page 63.

Skill Level

Beginner

Size

4½ inches W x
13½ inches H,
excluding hanger

Hop, buzz, sing and fly with this cheerful decoration. It's sure to put you in a summer-time mood!

COLOR KEY	
Plastic Canvas Yarn	**Yards**
■ Black #00	3
■ Red #01	2
■ Tangerine #11	3
□ Pumpkin #12	1
■ Fern #23	6
□ White #41	2
■ Watermelon #55	2
■ Bright purple #64	3
Uncoded area on frog is lemon #20 Continental Stitches	3
Uncoded area on bird is sail blue #35 Continental Stitches	3
⁄ Sail blue #35 Overcasting	
⁄ Mermaid #53 Overcasting	1
#3 Pearl Cotton	
⁄ Black Backstitch and Straight Stitch	1
⁄ Orange Straight Stitch	1
● Blue French Knot	1
● Black French Knot	
Color numbers given are for Uniek Needloft plastic canvas yarn.	

Spring Fling Wall Ornament
29 holes x 89 holes
Cut 1

Design by
Michele Wilcox

Ladybug Basket

Design by
Michele Wilcox

Skill Level

Beginner

Size

7 inches W x
9½ inches H

Picnic lunches will be much more fun when you bring along this sweet basket full of perky ladybugs!

Materials

- 1¼ sheets 7-count plastic canvas
- Uniek Needloft plastic canvas yarn as listed in color key
- #3 pearl cotton as listed in color key
- #16 tapestry needle
- Hot-glue gun

Instructions

1. Cut plastic canvas according to graphs. Cut one 45-hole x 29-hole piece for bottom. Bottom will remain unstitched.

2. Stitch pieces following graphs, working uncoded areas with fern Continental Stitches.

3. When background stitching is completed, work embroidery with black pearl cotton.

4. Using fern throughout, Overcast handle and top edges of front, back and sides. Whipstitch front and back to sides, then Whipstitch front, back and sides to bottom.

5. Referring to photo for placement, glue ends of handle (shaded gray) to inside edges of front and back. ✄

COLOR KEY	
Plastic Canvas Yarn	**Yards**
■ Black #00	6
■ Red #01	24
■ Forest #29	64
Uncoded areas are fern #23 Continental Stitches	45
╱ Fern #23 Overcasting	
#3 Pearl Cotton	
╱ Black Backstitch and Straight Stitch	8
● Black French Knot	
Color numbers given are for Uniek Needloft plastic canvas yarn.	

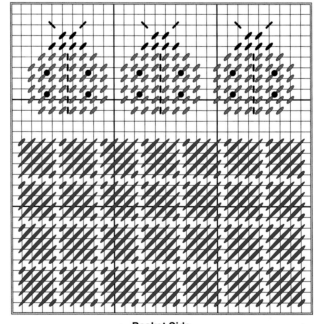

Basket Side
29 holes x 29 holes
Cut 2

Basket Handle
9 holes x 90 holes
Cut 1

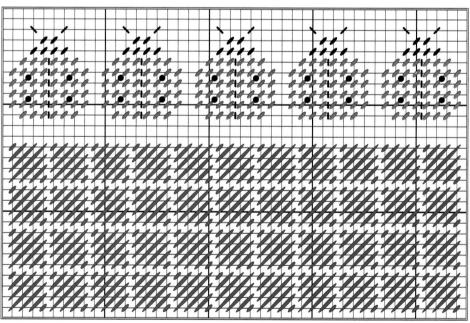

Basket Front & Back
45 holes x 29 holes
Cut 2

Napkin Ring Blossoms

Skill Level
Beginner

Size
Designs range from 3¾ inches W x 3⅜ inches H x 1¾ inches in diameter to 4 inches W x 4¼ inches H x 1¾ inches in diameter

Stitching these floral cuties will bring the warmth and freshness of the outdoors right to your table.

Designs by Carol Dace

Materials
- 1 sheet soft 7-count plastic canvas
- Worsted weight yarn as listed in color key
- #16 tapestry needle
- 4 silk flowers at least 3¼ inches in diameter
- 4 (10-inch) lengths ⅛-inch-wide satin ribbon to match silk flowers
- Glue gun

Project Note
Samples have a different color of yarn for hair on each ring. The yardage needed for hair on one ring is approximately 2 yards.

Instructions
1. Cut plastic canvas according to graphs.

2. Stitch ring following graph, overlapping three holes as indicated before stitching; Overcast edges. Stitch and Overcast leaves, using two stitches per hole where indicated.

3. Stitch and Overcast faces, working uncoded areas with light peach Continental Stitches. Use hair color desired to Overcast around sides and top where indicated.

4. Use 2 plies pink to work French Knot nose, wrapping yarn around needle once.

5. Using 1 ply yarn throughout, outline eyes and make brows with black. Stitch mouth with rose, wrapping yarn around needle once for French Knot.

6. For hair, work Turkey Loop Stitches as desired around sides and top of face, making loops from ⅜-inch to ⅝-inch long.

7. For each napkin ring, remove plastic center and stem from silk flowers and discard. Glue sections of flower around face. Glue two leaves to ring, then glue face with flower on top of leaves.

8. Tie each ribbon in a bow. Glue one bow to bottom of each face. ✄

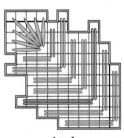

Leaf
11 holes x 11 holes
Cut 8

COLOR KEY

	Worsted Weight Yarn	Yards
⬜	Green	25
⬜	Pink	1
⬜	White	1
⬛	Black	1
	Uncoded areas are light peach Continental Stitches	4
╱	Hair color Overcasting	2 each
╱	Light peach Overcasting	
╱	Black Backstitch (1-ply)	
╱	Rose Straight Stitch (1-ply)	1
○	Pink French Knot (2-ply)	
●	Rose French Knot (1-ply)	

Napkin Ring
39 holes x 7 holes
Cut 4

Overlap   Overlap

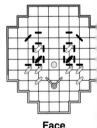

Face
9 holes x 10 holes
Cut 4

Gardener Frog Peg Rack

Skill Level

Intermediate

Size

8⅞ inches W x
8½ inches H x
1¾ inches D

This cute little frog will be hopping and hoeing his way into your heart!

Design by Janelle Giese

Materials

- 1 sheet stiff 7-count plastic canvas
- Uniek Needloft plastic canvas yarn as listed in color key
- #5 pearl cotton as listed in color key
- #16 tapestry needle
- Small amount light yellow-green 6-strand embroidery floss
- 2 (1⅜-inch x ⅜-inch) wooden shaker pegs
- Ivory acrylic craft paint
- Paintbrush
- Varnish or acrylic sealer
- Sawtooth hanger
- Thick white glue

Instructions

1. Cut plastic canvas according to graphs.

2. Paint pegs with ivory acrylic paint. Allow to dry. Seal with varnish or acrylic sealer. Allow to dry.

3. Place frog pieces together, then stitch and Overcast as one, working uncoded areas on frog with bright green Continental Stitches and uncoded area on spade of shovel with silver Continental Stitches. Uncoded areas inside blue lines, around cutout holes, should remain unstitched at this time.

4. For each unstitched area at bottom of motif, place two peg reinforcements over area, matching edges of reinforcements with

Plastic Canvas Yarn   **Yards**

⬭	Lavender #05	4
◇	Pink #07	3
♡	Tangerine #11	1
⬭	Pumpkin #12	2
▽	Maple #13	1
⬭	Cinnamon #14	3
△	Fern #23	7
⬭	Christmas green #28	7
⬭	Sail blue #35	3
⬭	Baby blue #36	3
⬭	Gray #38	2
◇	Eggshell #39	4
⬭	Beige #40	4
⬭	Purple #46	2
■	Turquoise #54	2
⬭	Yellow #57	3
♥	Bright purple #64	2
	Uncoded area on shovel is silver #37 Continental Stitches	2
	Uncoded areas on frog are bright green #61 Continental Stitches	5
⬭	Eggshell #39 Straight Stitch	

#5 Pearl Cotton

⟋	Black (1-strand) Backstitch and Straight Stitch	14
⟋	Black (2-strand) Backstitch	

Color numbers given are for Uniek Needloft plastic canvas yarn.

blue lines, then stitch through all thicknesses. *Note: The yellow stitch at each corner of openings are the only stitches at the center. Do not Overcast opening.*

5. Using black pearl cotton, work details on motif, using two strands where indicated and passing over each eye four times for pupils.

6. Use 1 strand eggshell to work eye highlight, splitting center of pupils.

7. Attach sawtooth hanger to backside just below nose with light yellow-green floss.

8. Apply a moderate amount of glue to peg ends, then twist and push pegs into openings; allow to dry. ✂

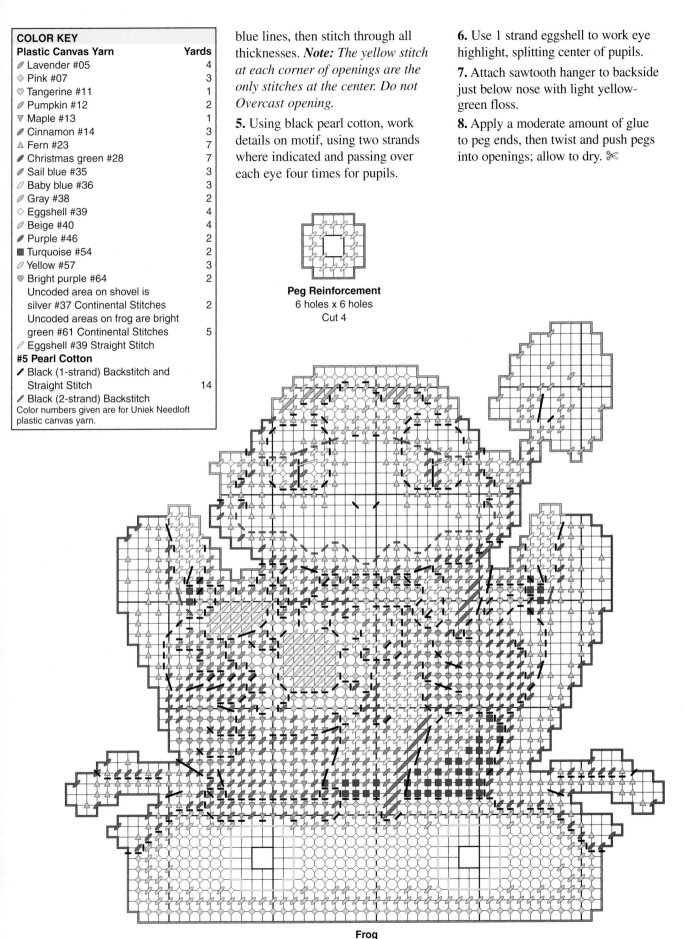

Peg Reinforcement
6 holes x 6 holes
Cut 4

Frog
58 holes x 56 holes
Cut 2, stitch as 1

Sunflower Birdhouse

Skill Level

Beginner

Size

6⅛ inches W x 6½ inches H x 5⅞ inches D

Irresistibly cheerful, this charming birdhouse will brighten your summer days!

Design by
Angie Arickx

Materials

- 1 artist-size sheet 7-count plastic canvas
- Uniek Needloft plastic canvas yarn as listed in color key
- #16 tapestry needle
- Hot-glue gun

Instructions

1. Cut plastic canvas according to graphs (this page and pages 69 and 71), cutting out hole on front only, leaving back intact. Cut one 29-hole x 29-hole piece for birdhouse bottom; leave unstitched.

2. Following graphs, Overcast fences. Stitch and Overcast sunflowers, window box and shutters.

3. Stitch remaining pieces following graphs. Overcast top edges of front, back and sides, and inside edges of front. Overcast bottom edges of roof sides and bottom edges roof trim from yellow dot to yellow dot.

4. Whipstitch birdhouse front and back to sides, then Whipstitch unstitched bottom to front, back and sides. Whipstitch top edges of roof sides together; tack roof sides to birdhouse front and back where indicated with red dots. Reinforce at tacking points with glue.

5. Whipstitch top edges of roof trim to roof side edges.

6. Using photo as a guide, glue shutters and window box around opening on front. Glue fences to front, back and sides, making sure bottom edges are even. Glue sunflowers to fences where indicated with blue dots. ✂

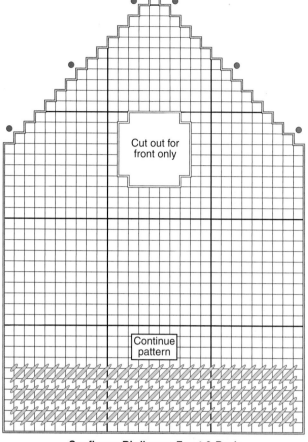

Sunflower Birdhouse Front & Back
29 holes x 41 holes
Cut 2

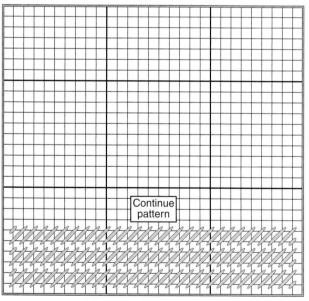

Sunflower Birdhouse Side
29 holes x 27 holes
Cut 2

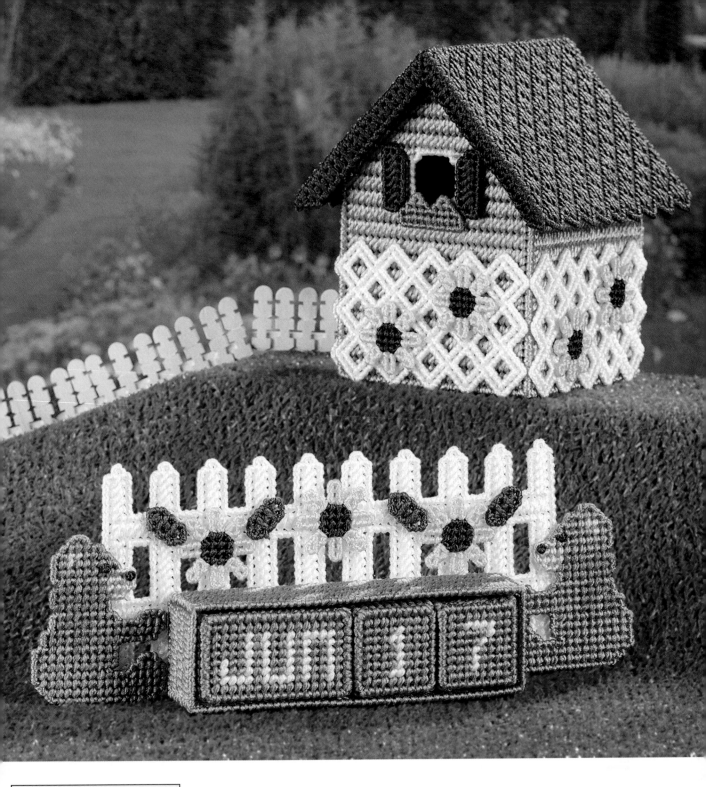

Sunflower
9 holes x 9 holes
Cut 8 for Sunflower Birdhouse
Cut 3 for Summer Block Calendar

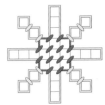

Window Box
9 holes x 4 holes
Cut 1

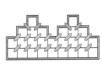

Shutter
3 holes x 8 holes
Cut 2

Graphs continued on page 71

Summer Sparkles **69**

Summer Block Calendar

Skill Level
Beginner

Size
11⅜ inches W x
4 ⅛ inches H x
1⅞ inches D

You'll love the practical beauty of this clever and decorative seasonal calendar!

Design by
Angie Arickx

Materials
- 1 sheet 7-count plastic canvas
- Uniek Needloft plastic canvas yarn as listed in color key
- #16 tapestry needle
- Hot-glue gun

Project Note
Some graphs are shared with similar calendars in other chapters of this book. Colors used for each season are given with the graphs and/or the instructions for that season.

Instructions

1. Following graphs throughout, cut box short sides, box long sides, box back, day blocks, fence and leaves (pages 32, 33 and 34); cut bears, sunflowers and month blocks (this page and pages 69 and 71).

2. Cut one 17-hole x 9-hole piece for month block side and two 9-hole x 9-hole pieces for month block ends; stitch all three pieces with fern Continental Stitches.

3. Stitch and Overcast fence, bears, sunflowers and leaves, working uncoded areas on bears with camel Continental Stitches. Stitch remaining pieces, working uncoded areas on block pieces with fern Continental Stitches. Uncoded area on box back should remain unstitched.

4. Work French Knots on bears when background stitching is completed. Overcast one long edge of each box side.

5. Using fern through step 7, Whipstitch box back to remaining long edges of box sides, then Whipstitch box long sides to box short sides.

6. Whipstitch the four month-block sides together along long edges, then Whipstitch month-block ends to sides.

7. For each day block, Whipstitch six pieces together, making sure there is one each of numbers "0," "1" and "2" with each block.

8. Making sure bottom edges are even, center and glue box back to fence, and bears to fence on each side of box. Glue sunflowers and leaves to fence above box. Place month and day blocks in box. ✂

See photo on page 69.

COLOR KEY	
Plastic Canvas Yarn	**Yards**
■ Brown #15	2
■ Fern #23	43
Holly #27	2
□ Beige #40	1
□ White #41	24
□ Yellow #57	3
■ Bright purple #64	2
Uncoded areas on bears are camel #43 Continental Stitches	6
Uncoded areas on block pieces are fern #23 Continental Stitches	
⁄ Camel #43 Overcasting	
● Brown #15 French Knot	
Color numbers given are for Uniek Needloft plastic canvas yarn.	

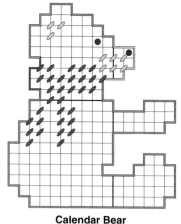

Calendar Bear
16 holes x 19 holes
Cut 2, reverse 1

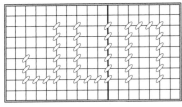

June Month Block Side
17 holes x 9 holes
Cut 1

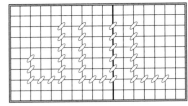

July Month Block Side
17 holes x 9 holes
Cut 1

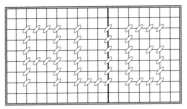

August Month Block Side
17 holes x 9 holes
Cut 1

Sunflower Birdhouse

Continued from page 69

COLOR KEY	
Plastic Canvas Yarn	**Yards**
▨ Maple #13	1
■ Brown #15	3
▨ Moss #25	50
■ Forest #29	37
▨ Mermaid #53	1
▨ Watermelon #55	1
☐ Yellow #57	7
╱ White #41 Overcasting	24
Color numbers given are for Uniek Needloft plastic canvas yarn.	

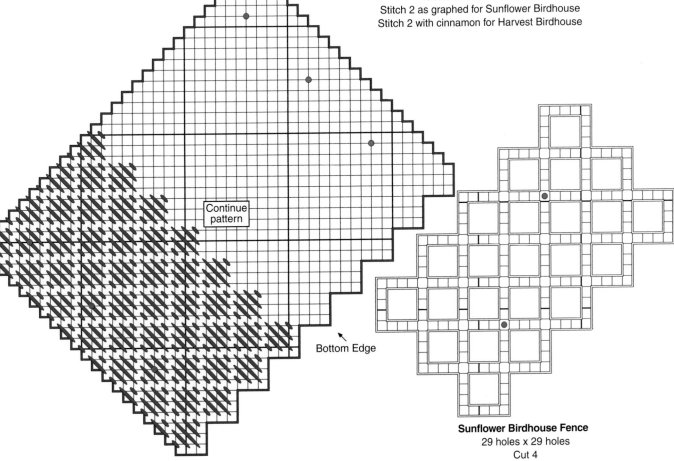

Birdhouse Roof Trim
39 holes x 20 holes
Cut 2 for each birdhouse
Stitch 2 as graphed for Sunflower Birdhouse
Stitch 2 with cinnamon for Harvest Birdhouse

Continue pattern

Bottom Edge

Roof Side
46 holes x 46 holes
Cut 2 for each birdhouse
Stitch 2 as graphed for Sunflower Birdhouse
Stitch 2 with cinnamon for Harvest Birdhouse

Sunflower Birdhouse Fence
29 holes x 29 holes
Cut 4

Summer Sparkles **71**

Uncle Sam Shelf Sitter

Skill Level
Intermediate

Size
10⅛ inches W x
8½ inches H x
2¾ inches D

This 3-D Uncle Sam takes a bow to help you show your patriotic pride!

Design by
Christina Laws

Materials
- 1½ sheets 7-count plastic canvas
- Worsted weight yarn as listed in color key
- #16 tapestry needle
- 2 (9mm) movable eyes
- Potpourri or polyester fiberfill
- Hot-glue gun

Instructions
1. Cut plastic canvas according to graphs (pages 73 and 77).

2. Stitch and Overcast sign, arms, mustache and nose following graphs, working uncoded background on sign with red Continental Stitches. When background stitching is completed, work Backstitches around letters with 2 plies blue.

3. Stitch head, body and back legs following graphs, working uncoded areas on back legs with black reverse continental stitches; work front legs reversing all stitches and leaving area between blue lines unstitched.

4. Whipstitch wrong sides of head front and back together following graphs. Using photo as a guide, glue mustache and eyes to head front, then glue nose to center top of mustache.

5. Using blue, Whipstitch edges between arrows on both ends of body top (this edge is the back edge of body top) to right side of front legs along blue lines. Place wrong sides of front and back legs together and continue Whipstitching legs to remaining back edges of body top through all three thicknesses.

6. Following graph, Whipstitch remaining edges of front and back legs together, Whipstitching back edge of body base to bottom edges of legs between blue lines.

7. Using blue, Whipstitch base to side edges body top, then Whipstitch body front to body top and bottom, filling with potpourri or fiberfill before closing.

8. Using photo as a guide, glue arms to front. Center and glue head on top of arms to front. Glue sign to backside of hands. ✂

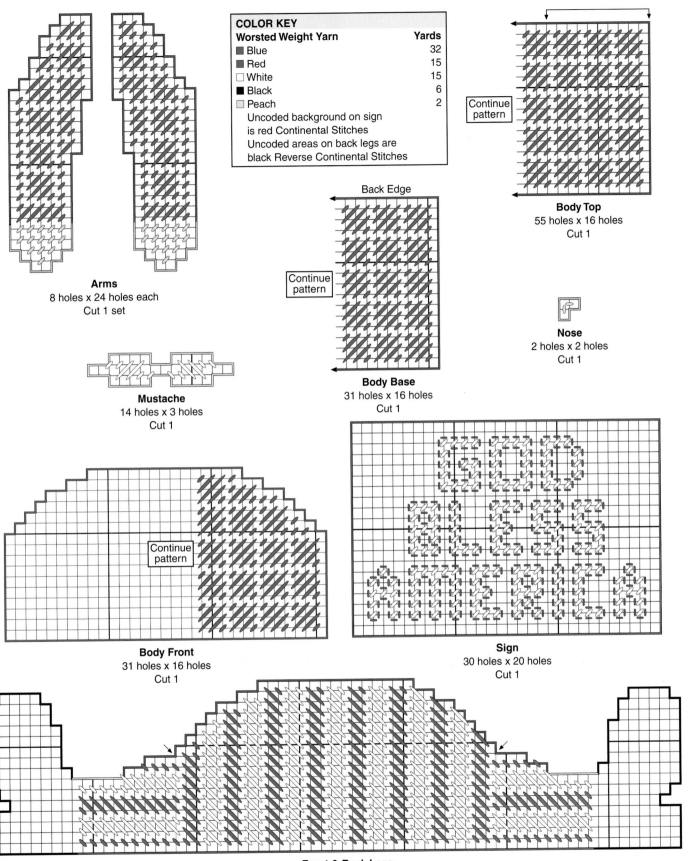

COLOR KEY

Worsted Weight Yarn	Yards
■ Blue	32
■ Red	15
□ White	15
■ Black	6
▨ Peach	2

Uncoded background on sign
is red Continental Stitches
Uncoded areas on back legs are
black Reverse Continental Stitches

Arms
8 holes x 24 holes each
Cut 1 set

Continue pattern

Body Top
55 holes x 16 holes
Cut 1

Back Edge

Continue pattern

Body Base
31 holes x 16 holes
Cut 1

Nose
2 holes x 2 holes
Cut 1

Mustache
14 holes x 3 holes
Cut 1

Continue pattern

Body Front
31 holes x 16 holes
Cut 1

Sign
30 holes x 20 holes
Cut 1

Front & Back Legs
67 holes x 16 holes
Cut 2
Stitch back legs as graphed
Stitch front legs, reversing stitches and eliminating
stitches in center area between blue lines

Graphs continued on page 77

Growing Patriots Flowerpot

Skill Level
Intermediate

Size
Flower: 3¼ inches W x 3 inches H

Leaves: 3 inches W x 1½ inches H

Assembled:
8¾ inches W x 11¼ inches H x 5 inches D

Sow the seeds of national pride with this friendly flowerpot!

Design by
Robin Howard-Will

Materials
- 2 sheets 7-count plastic canvas
- Coats & Clark Red Heart Super Saver worsted weight yarn Art. E301 as listed in color key
- #16 tapestry needle
- ³/₁₆-inch wooden dowel rods: 2 (10-inch), 3 (8-inch), 1 (6-inch)
- Hunter green acrylic craft paint
- Paintbrush
- 4½-inch clay flowerpot
- Floral foam to fit in 4½-inch pot
- Spanish moss
- Craft glue
- Glue gun

Instructions
1. Paint dowel rods with hunter green acrylic paint; allow to dry.

2. Cut plastic canvas according to graphs.

3. Stitch pieces following graphs, working two of flower C with cherry red as graphed and two with royal.

4. When background stitching is completed, embroider eyes and mouths on two each of flowers A and B for fronts. Work embroidery on one of each color for flower C. Do not embroider flower backs.

5. Overcast border, then work French Knots with 2 plies white. Cut two 8-inch lengths of royal blue yarn and tie one length to each end of border where indicated on graph with arrows.

6. Overcast leaves inside brackets; Overcast bottom edges of flowers from dot to dot. Whipstitch corresponding flower fronts and backs together. With wrong sides facing, Whipstitch remaining edges of leaves together.

7. Place floral foam in pot. Glue in place with craft glue; allow to dry.

8. Using hot glue, glue border to top of pot, then tie together tightly in back; trim ends.

9. Slide one set of leaves and one flower onto each rod. Push rods into floral foam as desired. Glue Spanish moss around flowers to cover foam. ✂

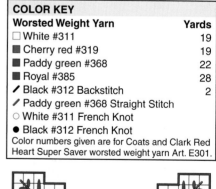

COLOR KEY

Worsted Weight Yarn	Yards
☐ White #311	19
■ Cherry red #319	19
■ Paddy green #368	22
■ Royal #385	28
╱ Black #312 Backstitch	2
╱ Paddy green #368 Straight Stitch	
○ White #311 French Knot	
● Black #312 French Knot	

Color numbers given are for Coats and Clark Red Heart Super Saver worsted weight yarn Art. E301.

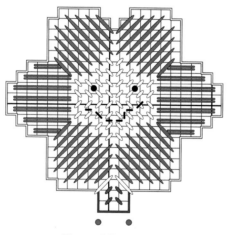

Flower C Front & Back
21 holes x 19 holes
Cut 4
Stitch 2 with cherry red
Stitch 2, replacing cherry red with royal
Stitch 1 of each color without embroidery for backs

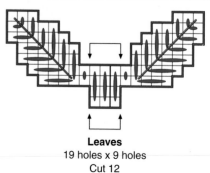

Leaves
19 holes x 9 holes
Cut 12

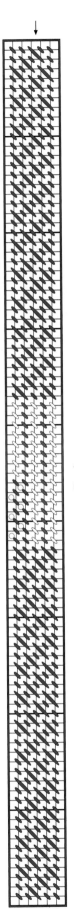

Border
90 holes x 6 holes
Cut 1

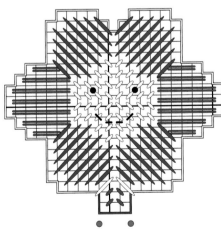

Flower A Front & Back
21 holes x 19 holes
Cut 4
Stitch 2 as graphed for fronts
Stitch 2 without embroidery for backs

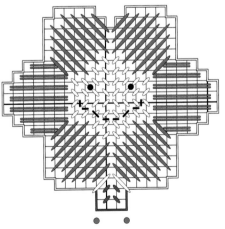

Flower B Front & Back
21 holes x 19 holes
Cut 4
Stitch 2 as graphed for fronts
Stitch 2 without embroidery for backs

Country Chicken Bucket

Skill Level
Beginner

Size
5⅛ inches W x
4¾ inches L x
7⅛ inches H

This friendly chicken is full of herself and will make you want to put all your eggs in one basket!

Design by
Judy Collishaw

Materials
- 1 sheet 7-count plastic canvas
- Worsted weight yarn as listed in color key
- DMC #5 pearl cotton as listed in color key
- #16 tapestry needle
- 2 (4mm) black round beads
- 5 (9-inch-long) strands natural raffia
- Hand-sewing needle
- Black sewing thread
- Glue gun

Instructions

1. Cut plastic canvas according to graphs. Cut one 28-hole x 14-hole piece for bucket base. Base will remain unstitched.

2. Stitch pieces following graphs, working uncoded areas with white Continental Stitches.

3. Work pearl cotton Backstitches on head when background stitching is completed. Using hand-sewing needle and black sewing thread, attach black beads to head where indicated on graph.

4. Overcast wings and top edges of sides. Overcast around top edges of front and back from dot to dot.

5. Whipstitch front and back to sides, then Whipstitch front, back and sides to unstitched base.

6. Using photo as a guide, glue wings to basket sides, placing wing edges inside brackets at an angle toward the front with rounded edges facing upward.

7. Place raffia lengths together and tie in a bow; glue to neck. ✂

COLOR KEY	
Worsted Weight Yarn	**Yards**
☐ White	30
▨ Gray	11
■ Red	1
☐ Yellow	1
Uncoded areas are white Continental Stitches	
⁄ White Straight Stitch	
#5 Pearl Cotton	
⁄ Light steel gray #318 Backstitch	1
⁄ Light pumpkin #970 Backstitch	1
● Attach black bead	
Color numbers given are for DMC #5 pearl cotton.	

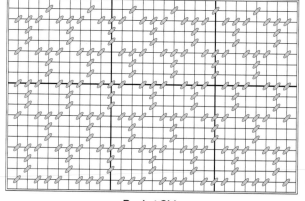

Bucket Side
28 holes x 18 holes
Cut 2

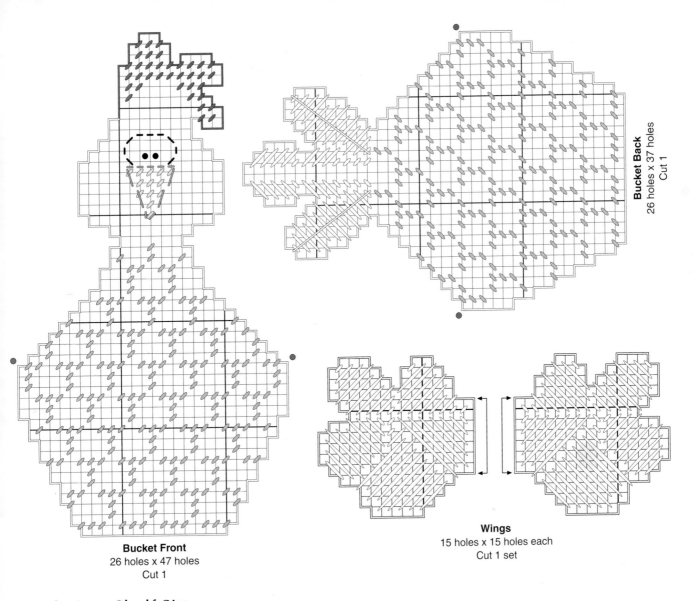

Bucket Back
26 holes x 37 holes
Cut 1

Bucket Front
26 holes x 47 holes
Cut 1

Wings
15 holes x 15 holes each
Cut 1 set

Uncle Sam Shelf Sitter

Continued from page 73

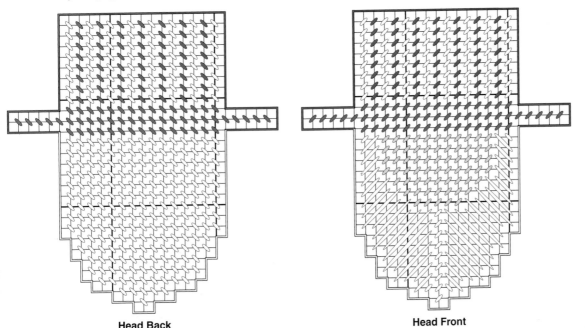

Head Back
26 holes x 28 holes
Cut 1

Head Front
26 holes x 28 holes
Cut 1

Summer Sparkles **77**

Cactus Kid Thermometer

Skill Level
Beginner

Size
5⅛ inches W x
10⅛ inches H,
excluding lasso

Keep this desert pal on the lookout to lasso those balmy summer days!

Materials
- ⅔ sheet 7-count plastic canvas
- Worsted weight yarn as listed in color key
- #16 tapestry needle
- 1-inch to 1½-inch x 5-inch to 5½-inch carded thermometer
- 2 (12mm) movable oval eyes
- ½-inch silver button with shank
- 8 inches natural jute
- Hand-sewing needle
- Black and beige sewing thread
- Glue gun

Instructions
1. Cut plastic canvas according to graphs.

2. Stitch and Overcast pieces following graphs, working uncoded areas on hat with light brown Continental Stitches and uncoded areas on bandanna with red Continental Stitches.

3. Sew silver button to hat where indicated on graph with sewing needle and black sewing thread.

4. Using photo as a guide through step 5, glue as follows to cactus: thermometer centered just above bottom edge, bandanna to "neck," hat to top of head at a slight angle, and eyes ½ inch above bandanna.

5. For lasso, roll natural jute into a couple of small loops and stitch to "hand" with sewing needle and beige sewing thread.

6. Hang as desired. ✂

Design by
Judy Collishaw

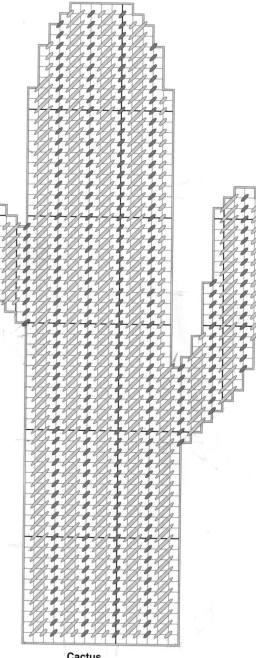

Cactus
34 holes x 60 holes
Cut 1

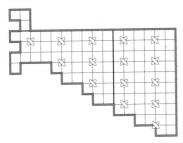

Bandanna
16 holes x 12 holes
Cut 1

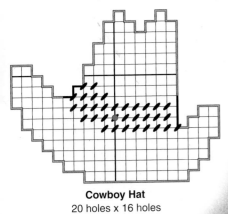

Cowboy Hat
20 holes x 16 holes
Cut 1

Butterfly & Flower Pokes

Skill Level
Beginner

Size
Butterfly Skewer:
3 inches W x
10 inches H

Flower Skewer:
3⅝ inches W x
10 inches H

Pretty and perky, these little pokes will brighten up any flowerpot!

Designs by
Ronda Bryce

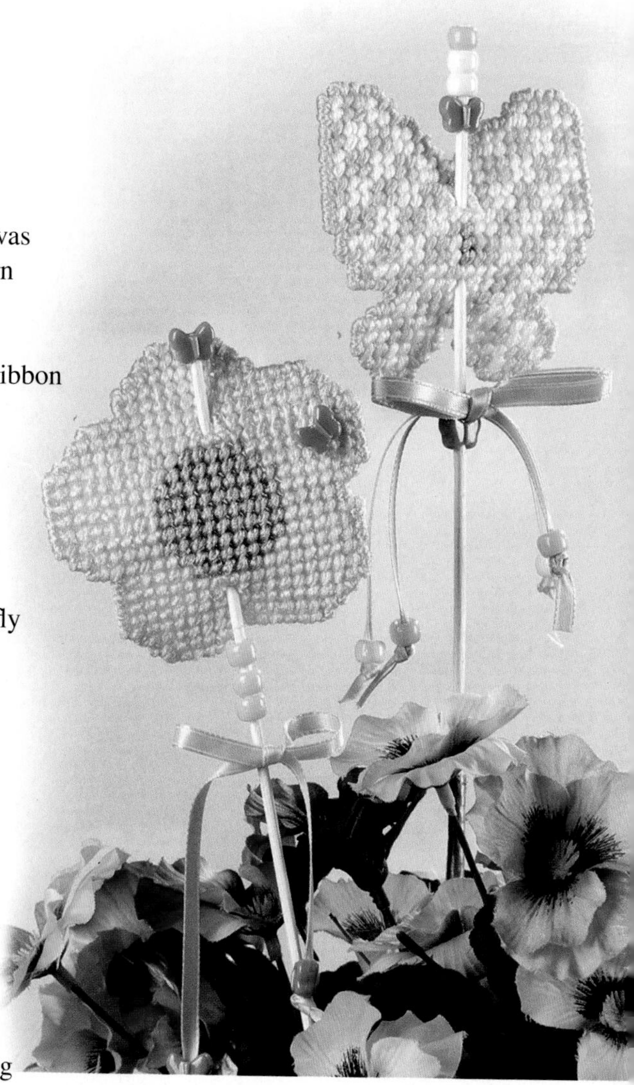

Instructions

1. Paint skewers with white acrylic paint; allow to dry.

2. Cut and stitch plastic canvas following graphs (page 85), working uncoded areas on butterfly with white Continental Stitches and uncoded areas on flower with lemon Continental Stitches.

3. Overcast inside edges on butterfly with white and inside edges on flower with lemon. Overcast outside edges on both pieces with yellow.

4. Cut yellow ribbon into two 18-inch lengths. Thread one white pony bead on each end of one yellow ribbon then tie a knot on each ribbon end. Repeat, threading one lavender butterfly bead on each end of remaining yellow ribbon and one yellow pony bead on each end of lavender ribbon.

5. For each poke, thread skewers through holes on pieces, allowing two inches of skewer above top hole in butterfly and one inch above top hole in flower.

6. Glue one butterfly bead to top of flower skewer. Thread and glue beads in the following order to top of butterfly skewer: one butterfly, two white, one yellow.

7. Thread and glue three yellow beads on skewer below flower, then tie yellow ribbon with butterfly beads in a bow below yellow beads. Using sewing needle and yellow sewing thread, attach butterfly bead to flower.

8. Place lavender ribbon and yellow ribbon with white beads together and tie in a bow around skewer below butterfly. Thread and glue remaining lavender butterfly bead on skewer below ribbon bow. ✄

Graphs continued on page 85

Happy Clowns Centerpiece

Materials

- 3 sheets 7-count plastic canvas
- Uniek Needloft plastic canvas yarn as listed in color key
- 6-strand embroidery floss as listed in color key
- #16 tapestry needle
- 8-inch x 10-inch oval wooden plaque from Walnut Hollow
- 12 (8mm) round red opaque beads
- ⅜-inch-wide ribbon: 68 inches red, 34 inches yellow
- Dental floss
- Small amounts regular felt: light yellow, deep pink, orange, light green
- 1½ sheets red self-adhesive felt
- Small amounts craft foam: red and yellow
- 2 (1½ -inch) colored round-head pins
- Acrylic craft paint: white and green
- 1-inch flat paintbrush
- 4 (1⅝ inch) lengths 18-gauge gold wire
- Hand-sewing needle
- Light pink sewing thread
- Needle-nose pliers
- Round toothpick
- Drill and drill bit size of toothpick
- Fiberfill
- Tacky craft glue
- Hot-glue gun

Preparation

1. Cut plastic canvas according to graphs (pages 84 and 85). Cut two 22-hole x 33 hole pieces for tall tent front and back.

2. Using patterns given (page 83), cut two clown hats from light yellow felt and one from deep pink. Cut one flag each from light green and orange felt.

3. Fold each flag in half around a colored round-head pin, placing flag directly under head of pin; glue felt together with tacky craft glue. Allow to dry; set aside.

4. Cut six ¼-inch circles each from red and yellow craft foam.

5. Shape hats into a cone and glue shut with tacky craft glue. When dry, stuff each with a small amount of fiberfill. Glue two red craft foam circles to front of each yellow hat and two yellow circles to deep pink hat. Glue one red bead to tip of each yellow hat. Set aside hats and remaining craft foam circles.

6. For base, paint top and sides of oval plaque with green acrylic paint. While paint is still moist, stipple with white paint (use clean brush to add small light dabs of white paint to surface). Allow to dry.

7. Drill hole in base top near front on left side where red clown will be positioned (see photo), drilling in ⅓ length of toothpick.

8. Adhere full sheet red self-adhesive felt to bottom of base; trim excess.

9. Cut 18 (¾-inch) circles from remaining red self-adhesive felt; cut circles in half. Beginning at center side of base (this will be front of centerpiece), adhere half circles around edge of base, making sure bottom edges are even and trimming down half circles as needed to fit at center back of base.

Clowns

1. Stitch clowns and feet following graphs, working uncoded areas on heads

Skill Level

Intermediate

Size

10½ inches W x
10¾ inches H x
8½ inches D

Bring your family into a playful state of mind with this trio of well-dressed clowns who will tumble, stumble and bumble all day!

Design by
Lee Lindeman

and hands with pink Continental Stitches. For blue and red clowns, stitch one clown as graphed; stitch remaining clown, replacing bright blue with Christmas red and yellow with tangerine.

2. When background stitching is completed, work French Knots for eyes with black floss. With hand-sewing needle and thread, attach one red bead to each face for nose

where indicated on graph. Using adjacent colors, fill in hair area with Turkey Loop Stitches, making loops approximately ¼-inch long.

3. Whipstitch wrong sides of corresponding clown fronts and backs together, stuffing with fiberfill before closing. Add more Turkey Loop Stitches over head edges if desired.

4. From yellow ribbon, cut four 6-inch lengths and one 10-inch length. From

red ribbon cut eight 6-inch lengths and two 10-inch lengths. Work a running stitch with dental floss along top edge of each length; draw floss to gather.

5. Using yellow ribbon for red clown and red ribbon for yellow and blue clowns, wrap 6-inch lengths around wrists and ankles (leave room for shoes) and 10-inch lengths around necks, tying and knotting off in back.

6. For each shoe, Whipstitch wrong

sides of two pieces together. Using photo as a guide, glue bottom edge of each leg to top of one shoe, so that toes extend out.

7. Using black embroidery floss, attach one red bead to toe of each shoe. For buttons, glue two red craft foam circles to front of yellow clown; glue two yellow craft foam circles each to fronts of red and blue clowns.

8. Glue yellow hat to top of yellow clown, glue deep pink hat to top of blue clown.

Box

1. Stitch top and sides following graphs, working one side each with yellow, bright blue, fern and turquoise, and two sides each with tangerine and red.

2. Using black, Whipstitch sides together, placing the red pieces on opposite sides and tangerine pieces on opposite sides. Whipstitch sides to top; Overcast bottom edges.

Tents

1. Stitch tall tent front and back with eggshell Continental Stitches. Stitch tent flap, all roof pieces and wide tent front and back following graphs,

working wide tent back entirely with eggshell Continental Stitches.

2. Overcast tent flap with eggshell and turquoise. Whipstitch wrong sides of corresponding tent pieces together; Overcast bottom edges. With right sides facing up, hot-glue eggshell edges of tent flap to diagonal edge of door on wide tent.

3. Whipstitch wrong sides of corresponding roof edges together around sides and top from dot to dot; Overcast bottom scalloped edges. Place roofs over tents; glue in place. Stuff tents with fiberfill.

4. Glue one flag pin in top of each roof with tacky glue.

Final Assembly

1. Using needle-nose pliers, bend each length of gold wire into a circle, interlocking them to form a chain. Before closing, thread

top circle through hole indicated on blue clown's hand; thread remaining bead on bottom circle.

2. Use photo as a guide and hot glue throughout assembly. Placing tall tent in back, glue tents close to back edge of base. Stuff box with fiberfill, then glue bottom edges to right side of base.

3. Glue blue clown to top of box. Glue yellow clown to left side near wide tent.

4. Insert ⅓ of toothpick in top of red clown's head. Cut off ⅓ from remaining end of tooth pick. Glue exposed end of toothpick in drilled hole, gluing top of head to base at same time. Glue remaining yellow hat to center front of base, near red clown. ✂

Flag
Cut 1 from orange felt
Cut 1 from light green felt

Clown Hat
Cut 2 from light yellow felt
Cut 2 from deep pink felt

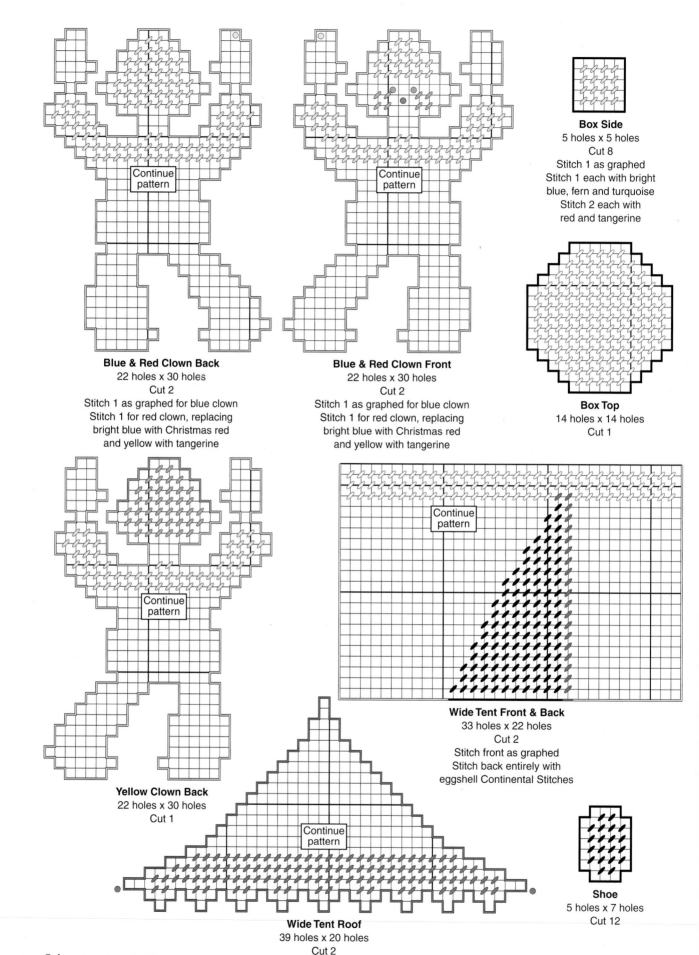

Blue & Red Clown Back
22 holes x 30 holes
Cut 2
Stitch 1 as graphed for blue clown
Stitch 1 for red clown, replacing
bright blue with Christmas red
and yellow with tangerine

Blue & Red Clown Front
22 holes x 30 holes
Cut 2
Stitch 1 as graphed for blue clown
Stitch 1 for red clown, replacing
bright blue with Christmas red
and yellow with tangerine

Box Side
5 holes x 5 holes
Cut 8
Stitch 1 as graphed
Stitch 1 each with bright
blue, fern and turquoise
Stitch 2 each with
red and tangerine

Box Top
14 holes x 14 holes
Cut 1

Yellow Clown Back
22 holes x 30 holes
Cut 1

Wide Tent Front & Back
33 holes x 22 holes
Cut 2
Stitch front as graphed
Stitch back entirely with
eggshell Continental Stitches

Wide Tent Roof
39 holes x 20 holes
Cut 2

Shoe
5 holes x 7 holes
Cut 12

Continue pattern

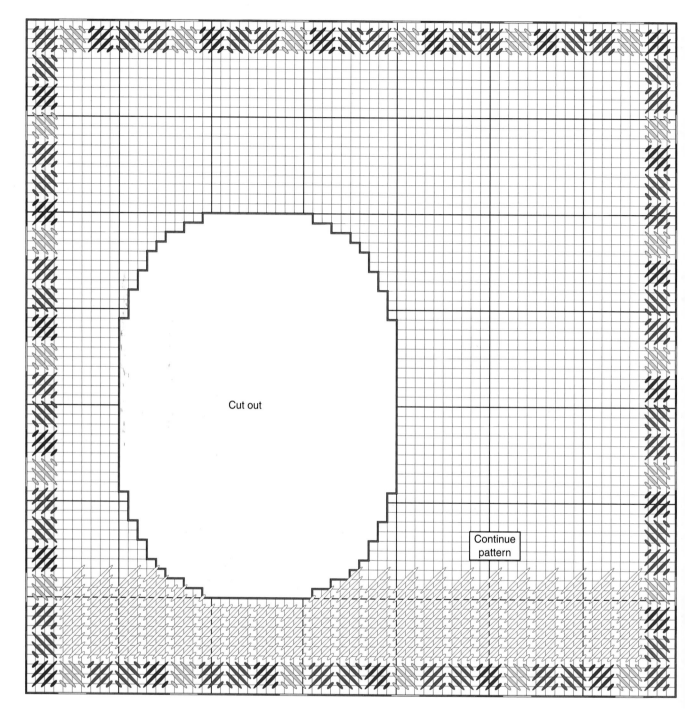

Frame
70 holes x 70 holes
Cut 1

Cut out

Continue pattern

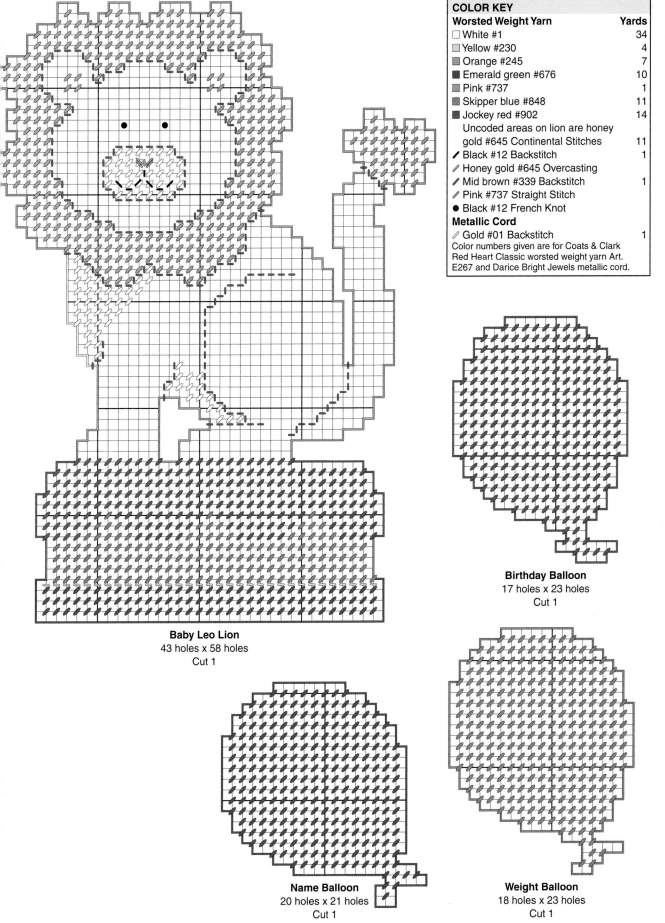

COLOR KEY

Worsted Weight Yarn	Yards
☐ White #1	34
☐ Yellow #230	4
▨ Orange #245	7
■ Emerald green #676	10
▨ Pink #737	1
▨ Skipper blue #848	11
■ Jockey red #902	14
Uncoded areas on lion are honey gold #645 Continental Stitches	11
╱ Black #12 Backstitch	1
╱ Honey gold #645 Overcasting	
╱ Mid brown #339 Backstitch	1
╱ Pink #737 Straight Stitch	
● Black #12 French Knot	
Metallic Cord	
╱ Gold #01 Backstitch	1

Color numbers given are for Coats & Clark Red Heart Classic worsted weight yarn Art. E267 and Darice Bright Jewels metallic cord.

Baby Leo Lion
43 holes x 58 holes
Cut 1

Birthday Balloon
17 holes x 23 holes
Cut 1

Name Balloon
20 holes x 21 holes
Cut 1

Weight Balloon
18 holes x 23 holes
Cut 1

Summer Sparkles **89**

Curious Kitten Coasters

Skill Level
Beginner

Size

Butterfly Kitten:
4¾ inches W x 5 inches H

Fishbowl Kitten:
4¾ inches W x 4¼ inches H

Toy Kitten:
4¾ inches W x 4⅜ inches H

Yarn Kitten:
4⅝ inches W x 4¾ inches H

Holder: 5⅛ inches W x 2⅜ inches H x 1⅛ inches D

Materials

- 2 sheets 7-count plastic canvas
- Worsted weight yarn as listed in color key
- #16 tapestry needle

Instructions

1. Cut plastic canvas according to graphs (this page and page 92). *Note: Cutout areas on yarn kitten are blue. All other cutout areas are white.* Cut one 33-hole x 7-hole piece for holder bottom. Holder bottom will remain unstitched.

2. Stitch and Overcast kittens with 4 plies yarn following graphs, working uncoded areas on butterfly, toy and yarn kittens with black Reverse Continental Stitches. Work uncoded areas on fishbowl kitten with gray Reverse Continental Stitches. *Note: Some edges on toy and yarn kittens will remain unstitched.*

3. Using 4 plies white throughout, work uncoded background on fence pieces with Continental Stitches. Overcast top edges from dot to dot and only the inside edges indicated. Remaining inside edges will not be stitched.

4. When background stitching and Overcasting are completed, stitch all embroidery on all pieces, working French Knots last and paying careful attention to number of plies used throughout.

5. Using 4 plies white, Whipstitch fence front and back pieces to side pieces, making sure to align cross bars and Overcasting remaining side edges where indicated. Using 4 plies green, Whipstitch front, back and sides to unstitched bottom. ✄

Capture the season of fun and frolic with these adorable kitty coasters!

Designs by Eunice Asberry

COLOR KEY

Plastic Canvas Yarn   Yards

☐	White
◼	Gray
◻	Orange
◻	Green
◼	Medium aqua
☐	Light aqua
◻	Pink

Uncoded background on fence is white Continental Stitches

Uncoded areas on butterly, toy and yarn kittens are black Reverse Continental Stitches

Uncoded areas on fishbowl kitten are gray Reverse Continental Stitches

✓ Black Overcasting and 2-ply Backstitch
✓ Black Backstitch (1-ply)
✓ Gray Straight Stitch (4-ply)
✓ Gray Backstitch (2-ply)
✓ Orange Backstitch and Straight Stitch (4-ply)
✓ Green Straight Stitch (4-ply)
✓ Green Backstitch and Straight Stitch (2-ply)
✓ Medium aqua Backstitch and Straight Stitch (2-ply)
⫽ Light aqua Straight Stitch (4-ply)
⫽ Light aqua Backstitch and Straight Stitch (2-ply)
⫽ Pink Backstitch (4-ply)
⫽ Pink Straight Stitch (2-ply)
● Black French Knot (2-ply)
○ Orange French Knot (2-ply)
● Medium aqua French Knot (2-ply)
○ Pink French Knot (2-ply)

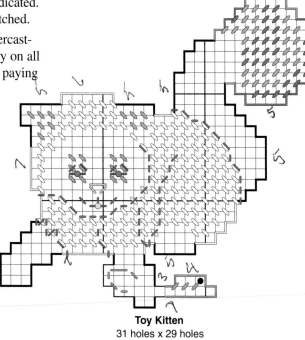

Toy Kitten
31 holes x 29 holes
Cut 1

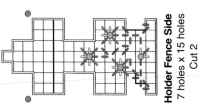

Holder Fence Side
7 holes x 15 holes
Cut 2

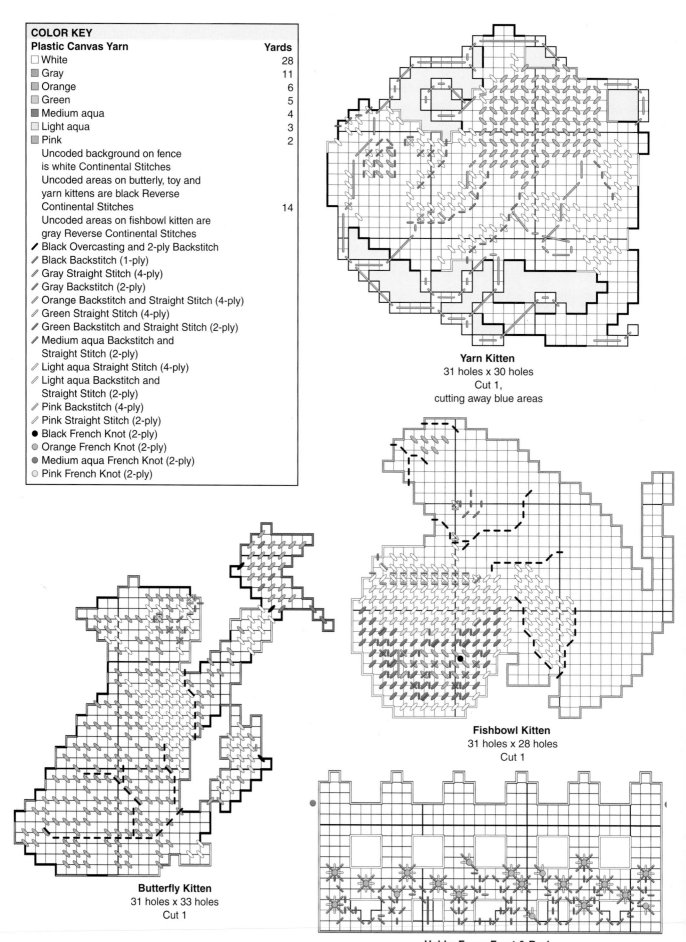

COLOR KEY

Plastic Canvas Yarn — Yards

□	White	28
▨	Gray	11
▨	Orange	6
▨	Green	5
▨	Medium aqua	4
□	Light aqua	3
▨	Pink	2

Uncoded background on fence
is white Continental Stitches
Uncoded areas on butterfly, toy and
yarn kittens are black Reverse
Continental Stitches — 14
Uncoded areas on fishbowl kitten are
gray Reverse Continental Stitches

⟋ Black Overcasting and 2-ply Backstitch
⟋ Black Backstitch (1-ply)
⟋ Gray Straight Stitch (4-ply)
⟋ Gray Backstitch (2-ply)
⟋ Orange Backstitch and Straight Stitch (4-ply)
⟋ Green Straight Stitch (4-ply)
⟋ Green Backstitch and Straight Stitch (2-ply)
⟋ Medium aqua Backstitch and
   Straight Stitch (2-ply)
⟋ Light aqua Straight Stitch (4-ply)
⟋ Light aqua Backstitch and
   Straight Stitch (2-ply)
⟋ Pink Backstitch (4-ply)
⟋ Pink Straight Stitch (2-ply)
● Black French Knot (2-ply)
○ Orange French Knot (2-ply)
● Medium aqua French Knot (2-ply)
○ Pink French Knot (2-ply)

Yarn Kitten
31 holes x 30 holes
Cut 1,
cutting away blue areas

Fishbowl Kitten
31 holes x 28 holes
Cut 1

Butterfly Kitten
31 holes x 33 holes
Cut 1

Holder Fence Front & Back
33 holes x 15 holes
Cut 2

Funky Bug Plaques

Materials

- 4 sheets 7-count plastic canvas
- Coats & Clark Red Heart Classic worsted weight yarn Art. E267 as listed in color key
- Coats & Clark Red Heart Kids worsted weight yarn Art. E711 as listed in color key
- 6-strand embroidery floss as listed in color key
- #16 tapestry needle
- #22 tapestry needle
- 10⅛-inch x 7½-inch rectangle each self-adhesive felt in black and red
- Picture hanger
- Hot-glue gun

Instructions

1. Cut one picture and three frames for each plaque from plastic canvas according to graphs (pages 95–97). Two frame pieces for each plaque will remain unstitched.

2. Stitch remaining pieces following graphs, working uncoded areas on frames with black Continental Stitches. Work uncoded areas inside blue lines on pictures with Continental Stitches as follows: butterfly with turquoise, dragonfly with yellow. Do not stitch on or outside blue lines on pictures.

3. When background stitching is completed, work French Knots on wings and antennae with yarn. With 6 strands black embroidery floss, work French Knots for eyes and Backstitches for mouths.

4. Matching outer edges, layer two unstitched frame pieces on each picture, then place a stitched frame on top. Working through all four thicknesses and using black yarn, Whipstitch inside edges of frame to picture at blue lines. Whipstitch outside edges through all thicknesses, using turquoise for butterfly and yellow for dragonfly.

5. Adhere red felt to back of butterfly plaque and black felt to back of dragonfly plaque. Glue picture hanger to center back near top edge. ✂

Full of bright color and cheery details, this peppy butterfly and sunny dragonfly will keep you smiling all summer long!

COLOR KEY	
Worsted Weight Yarn	**Yards**
☐ Yellow #230	32
☐ White #2001	12
■ Black #2012	56
☐ Orange #2252	4
■ Red #2390	6
☐ Lime #2652	10
☐ Pink #2734	12
■ Blue #2845	3
☐ Turquoise #2850	25
Uncoded area inside blue line on dragonfly picture is yellow #230 Continental Stitches	
Uncoded areas on frames are black #2012 Continental Stitches	
Uncoded area inside blue line on butterfly picture is turquoise #2850 Continental Stitches	
○ Yellow #230 French Knot	
○ Orange #2252 French Knot	
○ Lime #2652 French Knot	
○ Pink #2732 French Knot	
6-Strand Embroidery Floss	
╱ Black Backstitch and Straight Stitch	1
● Black French Knot	
Color numbers given are for Coats & Clark Red Heart Classic worsted weight yarn Art. E267 and Kids worsted weight yarn Art. E700.	

Funky Dragonfly
Plaque

94 *Too Cute! Plastic Canvas*

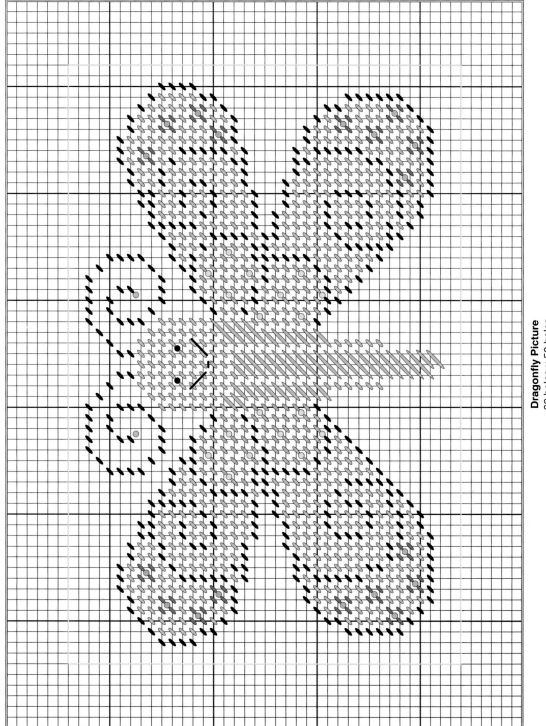

Dragonfly Picture
68 holes x 50 holes
Cut 1

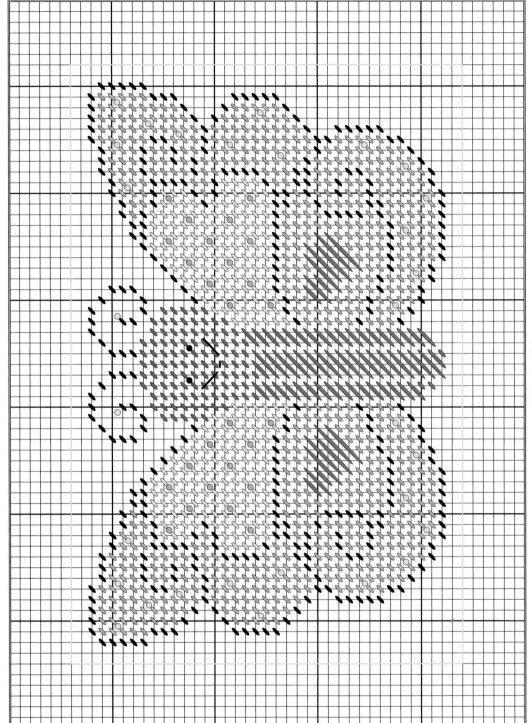

Butterfly Picture
68 holes x 50 holes
Cut 1

COLOR KEY

Plastic Canvas Yarn	Yards
■ Black #00	40
▢ Pink #07	4
▨ Pumpkin #12	56
☐ White #41	22

Uncoded areas on top and tail are pumpkin #12 Continental Stitches

6-Strand Embroidery Floss

╱ Black (8-ply) Backstitch and Straight Stitch	2
╱ Black (3-ply) Backstitch and Straight Stitch	
● Black (8-ply) French Knot	
○ Attach button	

Color numbers given are for Uniek Needloft plastic canvas yarn.

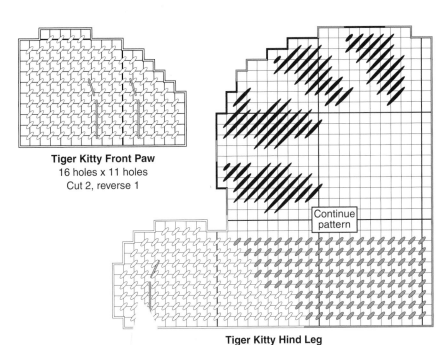

Tiger Kitty Front Paw
16 holes x 11 holes
Cut 2, reverse 1

Tiger Kitty Hind Leg
31 holes x 28 holes
Cut 2, reverse 1

Continue pattern

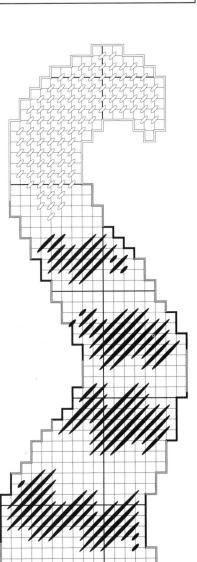

Tiger Kitty Tail
18 holes x 53 holes
Cut 1

Topper Front
33 holes x 45 holes
Cut 1

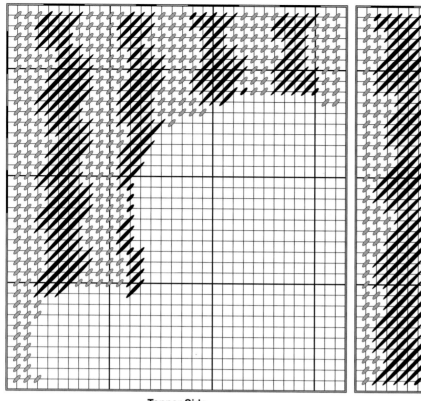

Topper Side
33 holes x 36 holes
Cut 2, reverse 1

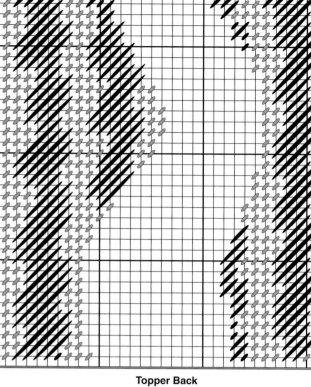

Topper Back
33 holes x 36 holes
Cut 1

Back Edge

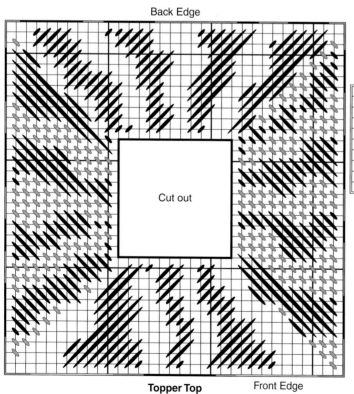

Cut out

Topper Top
33 holes x 33 holes
Cut 1

Front Edge

Tiger Kitty Muzzle
33 holes x 22 holes
Cut 1

COLOR KEY	
Plastic Canvas Yarn	**Yards**
■ Black #00	40
☐ Pink #07	4
▨ Pumpkin #12	56
☐ White #41	22
Uncoded areas on top and tail are pumpkin #12 Continental Stitches	
6-Strand Embroidery Floss	
⟋ Black (8-ply) Backstitch and Straight Stitch	2
⟋ Black (3-ply) Backstitch and Straight Stitch	
● Black (8-ply) French Knot	
○ Attach button	
Color numbers given are for Uniek Needloft plastic canvas yarn.	

Country Apples

Materials

- 4 sheets 7-count plastic canvas
- Worsted weight yarn: small amount light pink and as listed in color key
- #16 tapestry needle
- 8 inches magnetic strip
- Hot-glue gun

Country Apples Wall Hanging

1. Cut letter apples, seven medium apple leaves and two small apples from plastic canvas according to graphs (pages 107 and 109).

2. Stitch and Overcast pieces following graphs, working uncoded areas with off-white Continental Stitches. Do not work off-white straight stitches on small apples at this time.

3. Using photo as a guide, sew or glue leaves to letter apples.

4. Cut a 2-yard length of off-white yarn. Thread ends from back to front on both sides, then from front to back where indicated with blue lines on letter apple "C," pulling yarn completely through and keeping lengths even.

5. Continue threading on apples, spelling "COUNTRY." When completed, thread ends of yarn from back to front through holes indicated with blue dots on letter apple "Y." Tie yarn in a bow.

6. Using photo as a guide, use tails of yarn bow to work Straight Stitches on small apples; secure yarn on backside.

Basket Wall Hanging

1. Cut one basket, four apples, four medium apple leaves, four large apple blossom petals and two large apple blossom leaves from plastic canvas according to graphs (pages 107, 108 and 109).

2. Stitch and Overcast pieces following graphs, reversing two apples before stitching and working white highlight in same place on all four apples.

3. Following Fig. 1 (page 109), connect two blossom petals with light pink yarn. Place

remaining two petals between and slightly behind first two petals and connect with two light pink stitches, stitching over the connecting stitch of the first two petals.

4. Using photo as a guide, glue blossom leaves and blossom to lower left side of basket. Glue apple leaves to apples, then glue apples behind rim of basket.

Coasters

1. Cut four coaster apples, four coaster apple leaves, four small apple blossom petals and two small apple blossom leaves from plastic canvas according to graphs (pages 107, 108 and 109).

2. For coaster holder basket, cut one front, one back, one handle and two sides from plastic canvas according to graphs (pages 108). Cut one 18-hole x 6-hole piece for holder basket bottom which will remain unstitched.

3. Following graphs through step 5, stitch remaining pieces, working holder back entirely with tan Slanted Gobelin Stitches.

4. Overcast coaster apples, apple leaves, apple blossom leaves and apple blossom petals.

5. Overcast long edges of handles and top edges of holder front and back. Whipstitch front and back to sides, then Whipstitch front, back and sides to unstitched bottom. Whipstitch handle ends to top edges of sides.

6. Assemble apple blossom following step 3 of basket wall hanging. Using photo as a guide, glue blossom leaves and blossom to lower left side of holder.

7. Glue apple leaves to coaster apples. Place coasters in holder basket.

Magnets

1. Cut four magnet apples, four magnet apple leaves, four small apple blossom petals, two small apple blossom leaves, one holder basket front and one holder basket back from plastic canvas according to graphs (pages 107, 108 and 109).

2. Following graphs through step 4, stitch all pieces except holder back.

3. Overcast magnet apples, apple leaves, apple

blossom leaves and apple blossom petals.

4. Overcast top edges of holder back with tan. Overcast outside handle edges from dot to dot and all inside edges on holder front. Whipstitch unstitched holder back to side and bottom edges of holder front.

5. Assemble apple blossom following step 3 of basket wall hanging.

6. Using photo as a guide, glue blossom leaves and blossom to lower left side of holder. Sew or glue apple leaves to magnet apples.

7. Cut magnet strip into one ½-inch, one 3½-inch and four 1-inch lengths. Glue 1-inch length to backs of magnet apples, ½-inch length to back of basket handle and 3½-inch length to basket back.

8. Place apple magnets in holder basket. ✄

COLOR KEY	
Worsted Weight Yarn	**Yards**
■ Red	54
▨ Tan	40
□ Off-white	27
■ Green	12
■ Country blue	8
■ Brown	7
▨ Aquamarine	3
Uncoded areas on letter apples	
are off-white Continental Stitches	
⁄ Off-white Straight Stitch	

Large Apple Blossom Leaf
7 holes x 8 holes
Cut 2

Magnet Apple Leaf
3 holes x 4 holes
Cut 4

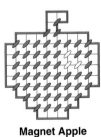

Magnet Apple
9 holes x 10 holes
Cut 4

Small Apple Blossom Leaf
5 holes x 7 holes
Cut 2 for coasters
Cut 2 for magnets

Medium Apple Leaf
5 holes x 6 holes
Cut 7 for country apples wall hanging
Cut 4 for basket wall hanging

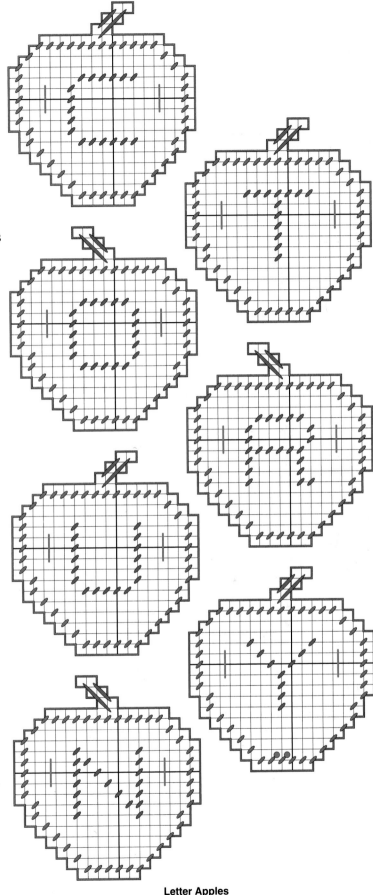

Letter Apples
18 holes x 19 holes
Cut 1 each

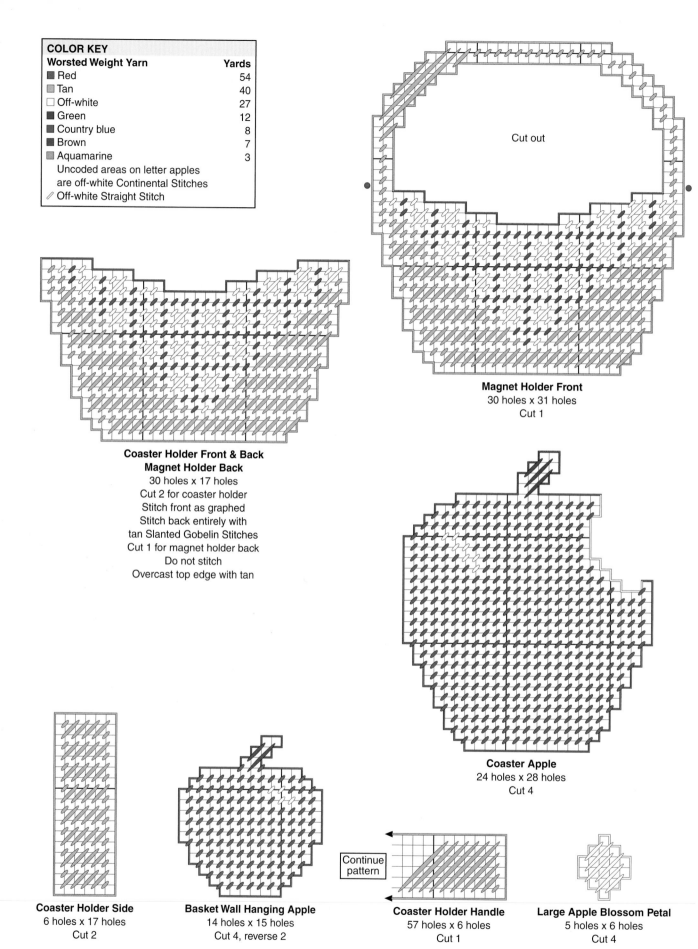

COLOR KEY

Worsted Weight Yarn	Yards
■ Red	54
■ Tan	40
□ Off-white	27
■ Green	12
■ Country blue	8
■ Brown	7
■ Aquamarine	3

Uncoded areas on letter apples
are off-white Continental Stitches

⁄ Off-white Straight Stitch

Magnet Holder Front
30 holes x 31 holes
Cut 1

Cut out

Coaster Holder Front & Back
Magnet Holder Back
30 holes x 17 holes
Cut 2 for coaster holder
Stitch front as graphed
Stitch back entirely with
tan Slanted Gobelin Stitches
Cut 1 for magnet holder back
Do not stitch
Overcast top edge with tan

Coaster Apple
24 holes x 28 holes
Cut 4

Coaster Holder Side
6 holes x 17 holes
Cut 2

Basket Wall Hanging Apple
14 holes x 15 holes
Cut 4, reverse 2

Continue
pattern

Coaster Holder Handle
57 holes x 6 holes
Cut 1

Large Apple Blossom Petal
5 holes x 6 holes
Cut 4

Small Apple Blossom Petal
3 holes x 4 holes
Cut 4 for coasters
Cut 4 for magnets

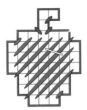

Small Apple
7 holes x 9 holes
Cut 2

Coaster Apple Leaf
5 holes x 8 holes
Cut 4

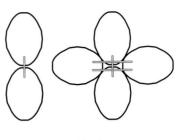

Fig. 1
Apple Blossom

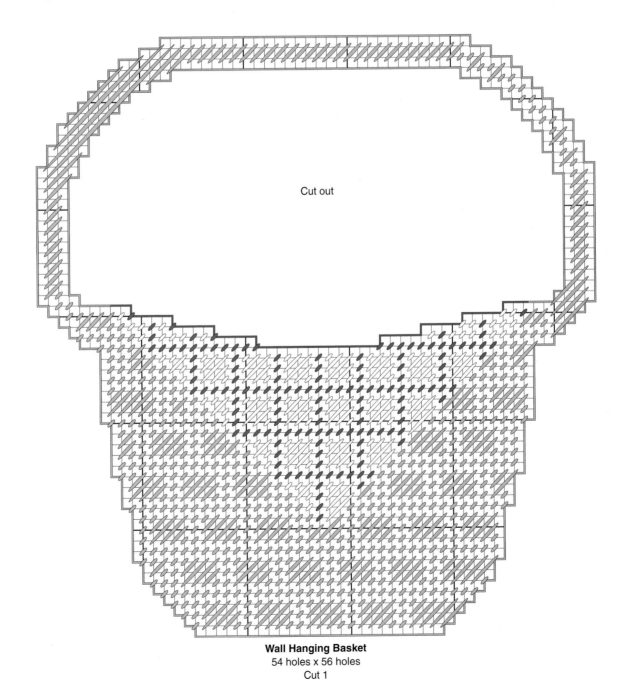

Cut out

Wall Hanging Basket
54 holes x 56 holes
Cut 1

Autumn Color **109**

Gourds for Sale Coaster Set

Skill Level

Intermediate

Size

Coaster: 5¾ inches W x 6 inches H

Wagon Holder: 8 inches W x 3 inches H x 3½ inches D

Celebrate the bounty of the autumn season with this whimsical wagon and cheerful gourd coasters!

Designs by Nancy Billetdeaux

Materials

- 2 sheets 7-count plastic canvas
- Worsted weight yarn as listed in color key
- #16 tapestry needle
- 4 (1¼-inch) wooden wheels
- Black glossy acrylic paint
- Paintbrush
- Hot-glue gun

Cutting & Stitching

1. Cut plastic canvas according to graphs (page 119).

2. Stitch and Overcast coasters and sign, working uncoded background on sign with brown Continental Stitches.

3. When background stitching is completed, work black Backstitches on coasters and orange Backstitches for letters on sign.

4. Stitch wagon pieces, working uncoded areas with black Continental Stitches. Overcast all but bottom edge of handle.

5. For top boards, Overcast bottom edges of two top side boards and two end boards; for middle boards, Overcast top and bottom edges of middle side boards and two end boards; for bottom boards, Overcast top edges of two bottom side boards and two end boards.

6. For middle vertical support boards, Overcast both side edges of two boards; for corner vertical support boards, Overcast one side edge. Top and bottom edges of support boards will remain unstitched at this time.

Assembly

1. Paint wheels black; allow to dry.

2. With wrong sides facing, place one top side board and one top end board together. Sandwich between them two corner vertical support boards (Fig. 1) so that wrong sides of top boards and support boards are facing; with top edges even, Whipstitch corner vertical edges together through all four thicknesses.

3. Whipstitch corner supports together for two more holes; place middle side board and middle end board on the outside of corner vertical supports along next four holes as indicated on vertical support board graph; Whipstitch through all four thicknesses.

4. Whipstitch corner vertical supports together for two more holes then attach bottom boards in same manner, making sure bottom edges are even.

5. Repeat for each corner of wagon.

6. Whipstitch top edges of corner vertical supports to top boards, Overcasting remaining top edges of wagon and Whipstitching middle supports to top side boards where indicated on graph.

7. Working through all thicknesses, Whipstitch wagon bottom to bottom boards and to corner and middle vertical supports, Whipstitching handle to one end board where indicated.

8. Using photo as a guide throughout, glue wheels to wagon, keeping wagon level. Glue sign to one side of wagon. Place coasters in wagon. ✂

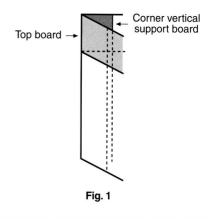

Fig. 1

Graphs continued on page 119

Autumn Block Calendar

Skill Level
Beginner

Size
11¾ inches W x
4⅛ inches H x
1⅞ inches D

From hayrides and hoedowns to a happy Thanksgiving, this practical calendar will keep track of all your autumn antics.

Design by
Angie Arickx

Materials

- 1 sheet 7-count plastic canvas
- Uniek Needloft plastic canvas yarn as listed in color key
- #16 tapestry needle
- Hot-glue gun

Project Note

Some graphs are shared with similar calendars in other chapters of this book. Colors used for each season are given with the graphs and/or the instructions for that season.

Instructions

1. Following graphs throughout, cut box short sides, box long sides, box back, day blocks and fence (pages 33 and 34); cut scarecrows, pumpkin, leaves and month blocks.

2. Cut one 17-hole x 9-hole piece for month block side and two 9-hole x 9-hole pieces for month block ends; stitch all three pieces with gold Continental Stitches.

3. Stitch and Overcast fence, scarecrows, pumpkin and leaves, reversing one scarecrow before stitching. Stitch remaining pieces, working uncoded areas on block pieces with gold Continental Stitches. Uncoded area on box back should remain unstitched.

4. Overcast one long edge of each box side.

5. Using gold through step 7, Whipstitch box back to remaining long edges of box sides, then Whipstitch box long sides to box short sides.

6. Whipstitch the four month block sides together along long edges, then Whipstitch month block ends to sides.

7. For each day block, Whipstitch six pieces together, making sure there is one each of numbers "0", "1" and "2" with each block.

8. Making sure bottom edges are even, center and glue box back to fence; with legs facing out, glue scarecrows to fence on each side of box. Center and glue pumpkin to fence above box; glue three leaves to fence on each side of pumpkin.

9. Place month and day blocks in box. ✂

COLOR KEY	
Plastic Canvas Yarn	**Yards**
☐ Rust #09	4
■ Cinnamon #14	3
■ Holly #27	3
☐ Eggshell #39	24
☐ Camel #43	1
■ Bittersweet #52	2
☐ Yellow #57	1
Uncoded areas are on block pieces are gold #17 Continental Stitches	43
⟋ Gold #17 Overcasting	
Color numbers given are for Uniek Needloft plastic canvas yarn.	

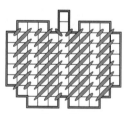

Pumpkin
11 holes x 9 holes
Cut 1

Pumpkin Leaf
4 holes x 4 holes
Cut 6

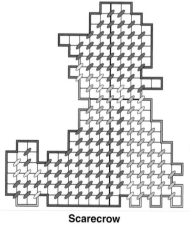

Scarecrow
17 holes x 19 holes
Cut 2, reverse 1

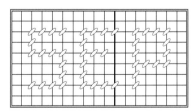

September Month Block Side
17 holes x 9 holes
Cut 1

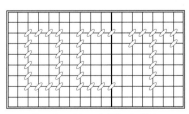

October Month Block Side
17 holes x 9 holes
Cut 1

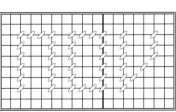

November Month Block Side
17 holes x 9 holes
Cut 1

Autumn Color **113**

Harvest Birdhouse

Skill Level

Beginner

Size

6¼ inches W x
9¼ inches H x
5⅞ inches D

With its bright fall colors and pumpkins aplenty, this charming birdhouse will warm your heart and home!

Materials

- 1¼ artist-size sheets 7-count plastic canvas
- Uniek Needloft plastic canvas yarn as listed in color key
- #16 tapestry needle
- Hot-glue gun

Instructions

1. Following graphs throughout, cut roof sides and roof trim (page 71); cut remaining pieces, cutting out holes on birdhouse front only, leaving back intact. Cut one 29-hole x 29-hole piece for birdhouse bottom. Bottom will remain unstitched.

2. Stitch and Overcast window boxes, shutters, pumpkins and trellises, reversing one trellis before stitching.

3. Stitch remaining pieces, filling in bottom panes of windows on birdhouse back (where holes are on front) the same as top window-panes stitching a row of eggshell Continental Stitches between panes.

4. Overcast top edges of front, back and sides, and inside edges of front. Overcast bottom edges of roof sides and bottom edges of roof trim from yellow dot to yellow dot.

5. Whipstitch birdhouse front and back to sides, then Whipstitch front, back and sides to unstitched bottom. Whipstitch top edges of roof sides together, tack roof sides to birdhouse front and back where indicated with red dots. Reinforce at tacking points with glue.

6. With cinnamon, Whipstitch top edges of roof trim to roof side edges.

7. Glue large shutters at sides of openings and windows on front and back; glue small shutters in place on birdhouse sides. Glue window boxes under openings and windows.

8. Center and glue one pumpkin to front along bottom edge. Glue two pumpkins each to back and sides. With grass at bottom, glue trellis pieces to left and right sides of front, making sure bottom edges are even. ✄

Design by
Angie Arickx

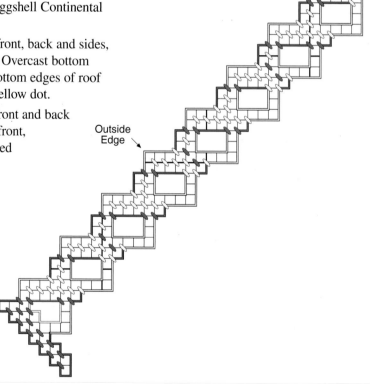

Outside Edge

Trellis
35 holes x 37 holes
Cut 2, reverse 1

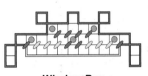

Window Box
13 holes x 5 holes
Cut 8

Small Shutter
3 holes x 7 holes
Cut 8

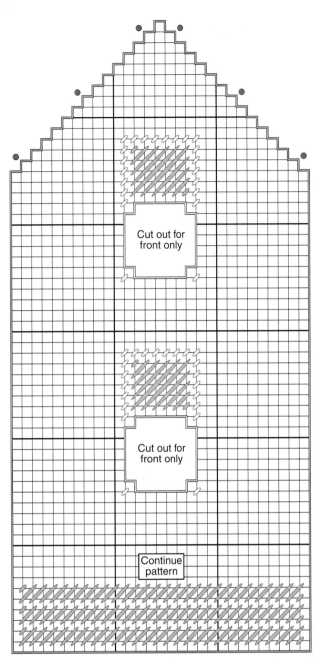

Harvest Birdhouse Front & Back
29 holes x 59 holes
Cut 2

Cut out for front only

Cut out for front only

Continue pattern

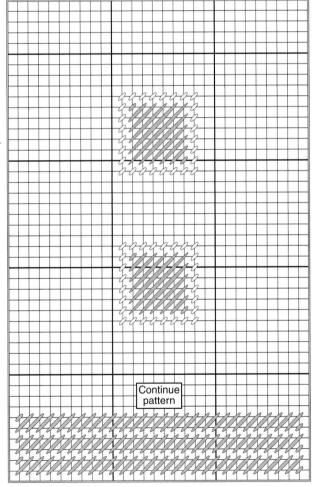

Continue pattern

Harvest Birdhouse Side
29 holes x 45 holes
Cut 2

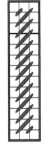

Large Shutter
3 holes x 13 holes
Cut 8

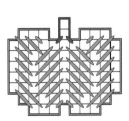

Pumpkin
11 holes x 9 holes
Cut 7

Sunflower Season Candleholder & Caddy

Skill Level

Beginner

Size

Caddy: 10¾ inches W x 6⅛ inches H x 4¼ inches D

Candleholder: 2½ inches H x 4 inches in diameter

Bring the breezy warmth of early fall indoors when you decorate your home with this bright and cheerful set!

Designs by Mary T. Cosgrove

Materials

- 1 sheet orange 7-count plastic canvas
- ¼ sheet clear plastic canvas
- Uniek Needloft plastic yarn as listed in color key
- #16 tapestry needle
- 3 (19½-inch) lengths ¼-inch-wide yellow satin ribbon
- Fabric glue

Project Note

Please use caution. Plastic canvas and plastic canvas yarn will melt and burn if it gets too hot or comes in contact with a flame. Never leave a lighted candle unattended.

Caddy

1. Cut caddy front, back and side pieces from orange plastic canvas; cut row of flowers from clear plastic canvas according to graphs (pages 117, 118 and 125). Cut one 70-hole x 27-hole piece from orange plastic canvas for caddy bottom. Bottom will remain unstitched.

2. Stitch row of flowers following graph, working uncoded centers with brown Continental Stitches.

3. Place row of flowers on caddy front where indicated with green and yellow lines; Whipstitch in place with Christmas green and yellow as indicated, Overcasting top edges of flowers while Whipstitching. Do not Whipstitch bottom edges together at this time.

4. Backstitch with bittersweet around flower centers, working through both thicknesses at bottom of flowers and working Straight Stitches over petal edges while Backstitching.

5. Using bittersweet, Whipstitch front and back to sides, then Whipstitch front, back and sides to bottom, catching bottom of leaves on row of flowers while Whipstitching.

6. Glue ribbon lengths around sides and back where indicated with shaded yellow areas, trimming as needed to fit. Work Christmas green Straight Stitches on sides and back over yellow ribbon.

Candleholder

1. Cut candleholder pieces from clear plastic canvas according to graphs (pages 118 and 125).

2. Stitch and Overcast candleholder flowers, working uncoded centers with brown Continental Stitches. Backstitch with bittersweet around flower centers, working bittersweet Straight Stitches over petal edges while Backstitching.

3. While stitching leaves, form a ring by overlapping the two pieces where indicated, placing the shaded green area under end of other side, then working stitches as indicated.

4. Using bittersweet, Whipstitch bottom edges of leaves to straight edges on holder bottom, Overcasting remaining edges of leaves while Whipstitching. Overcast remaining edges of bottom with brown.

5. Use bittersweet to tack flowers to leaves where indicated with orange dots on leaves (see photo), or use fabric glue if desired. ✂

COLOR KEY	
Plastic Canvas Yarn	**Yards**
■ Brown #15	10
■ Christmas green #28	14
■ Bittersweet #52	13
☐ Yellow #57	15
Uncoded flower centers are brown #15 Continental Stitches	
⁄ Christmas green #28 Straight Stitch	
⁄ Bittersweet #52 Backstitch and Straight Stitch	
Color numbers given are for Uniek Needloft plastic canvas yarn.	

Row of Flowers
60 holes x 39 holes
Cut 1 from clear

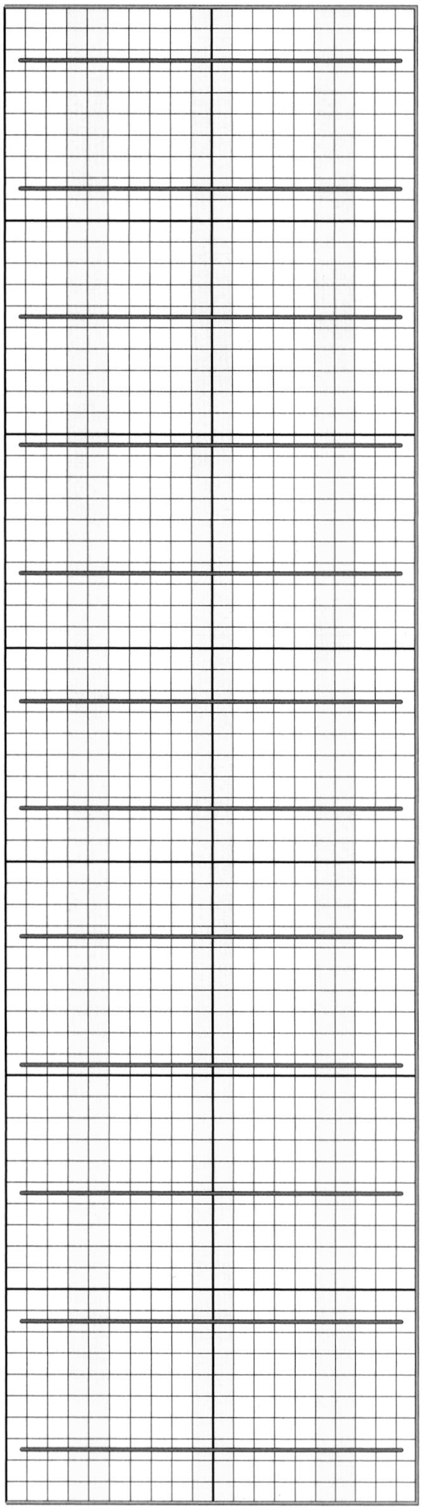

Caddy Back
70 holes x 20 holes
Cut 1 from orange

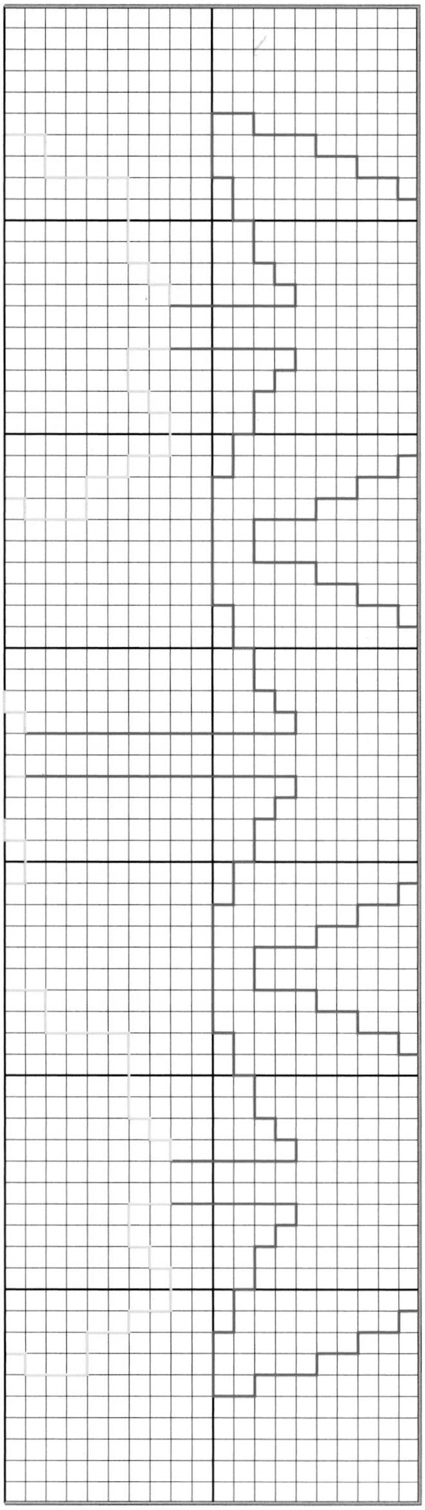

Caddy Front
70 holes x 20 holes
Cut 1 from orange

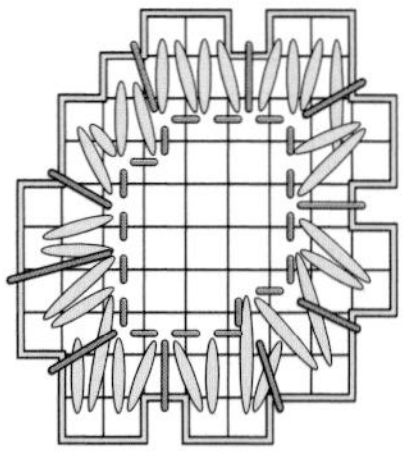

Candleholder Flower
9 holes x 10 holes
Cut 4 from clear

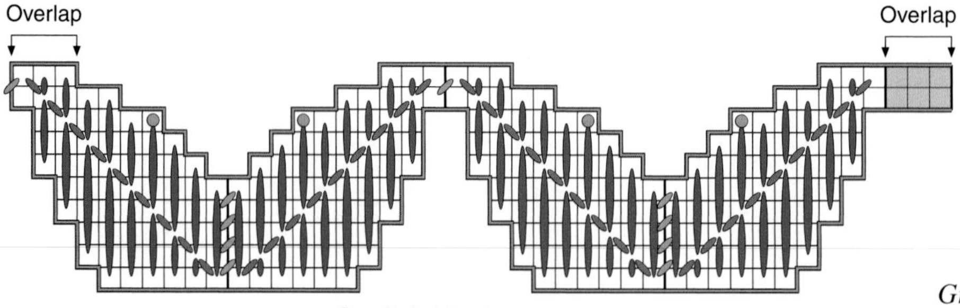

Overlap

Overlap

Candleholder Leaves
43 holes x 10 holes
Cut 2 from clear

Graphs continued on page 125

Gourds for Sale Coaster Set

Continued from page 110

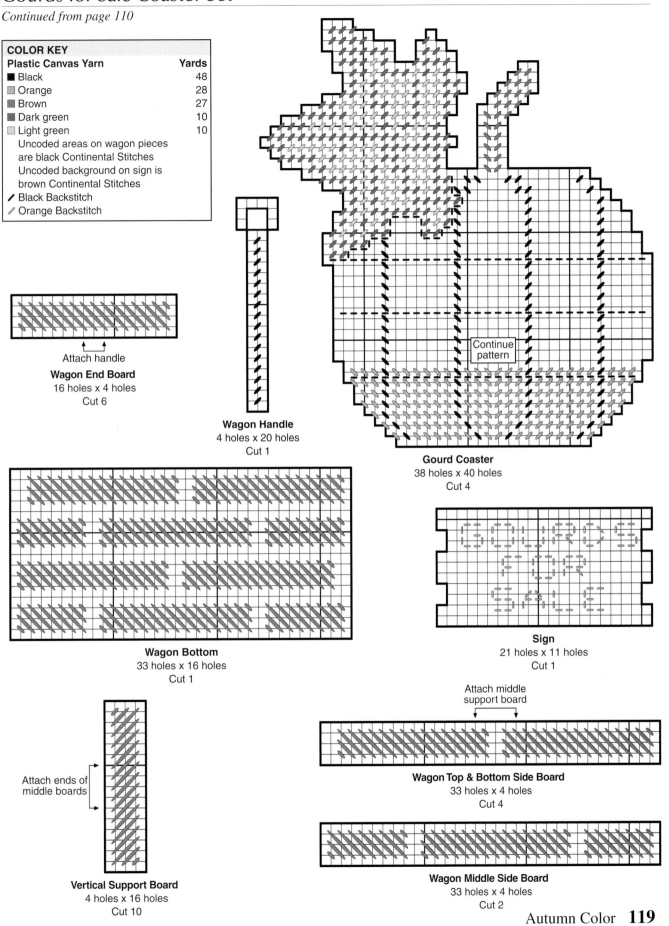

COLOR KEY

Plastic Canvas Yarn	Yards
■ Black	48
▦ Orange	28
▩ Brown	27
▨ Dark green	10
▢ Light green	10

Uncoded areas on wagon pieces
are black Continental Stitches
Uncoded background on sign is
brown Continental Stitches
✒ Black Backstitch
✒ Orange Backstitch

Wagon End Board
16 holes x 4 holes
Cut 6

Attach handle

Wagon Handle
4 holes x 20 holes
Cut 1

Continue
pattern

Gourd Coaster
38 holes x 40 holes
Cut 4

Wagon Bottom
33 holes x 16 holes
Cut 1

Sign
21 holes x 11 holes
Cut 1

Attach ends of
middle boards

Vertical Support Board
4 holes x 16 holes
Cut 10

Attach middle
support board

Wagon Top & Bottom Side Board
33 holes x 4 holes
Cut 4

Wagon Middle Side Board
33 holes x 4 holes
Cut 2

Ghostly Greetings

Skill Level
Beginner

Size
13½ W x 24 inches L

Materials
- 3 sheets 7-count plastic canvas
- Coats & Clark Red Heart Super Saver worsted weight yarn Art. E301 as listed in color key
- #16 tapestry needle
- 2 (12mm) printed movable eyes from Darice
- 1-inch white plastic ring
- Hot-glue gun

Instructions
1. Cut plastic canvas according to graphs (this page and pages 122 and 123). Ghost back pieces will remain unstitched.

2. Stitch ghost front pieces and bat following graphs, working uncoded areas on bat with black Continental Stitches.

3. When background stitching is completed, Backstitch with white for highlights on eyes. Using white yarn, center and attach white plastic ring to wrong side of head back about 11 holes from top; glue yarn to back to secure.

4. With white, Whipstitch top and bottom front pieces together at centers. Repeat for back pieces, then Whipstitch front and back together.

5. Overcast bat with black. Glue movable eyes to bat where indicated on graph. Glue bat to center of ghost, covering seam. ✂

Go a little "batty" on Halloween with this playfully mischievous ghost!

Design by Robin Howard-Will

COLOR KEY	
Worsted Weight Yarn	**Yards**
☐ White #311	82
■ Black #312	16
☐ Bright yellow #324	1
▨ Vibrant orange #354	2
Uncoded areas on bat are black #312 Continental Stitches	
✎ White #311 Backstitch	
● Attach movable eye	
Color numbers given are for Coats & Clark Red Heart Super Saver worsted weight yarn Art. E301 worsted weight yarn.	

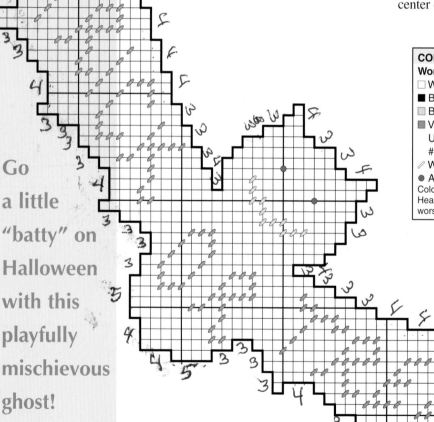

Bat
67 holes x 67 holes
Cut 1

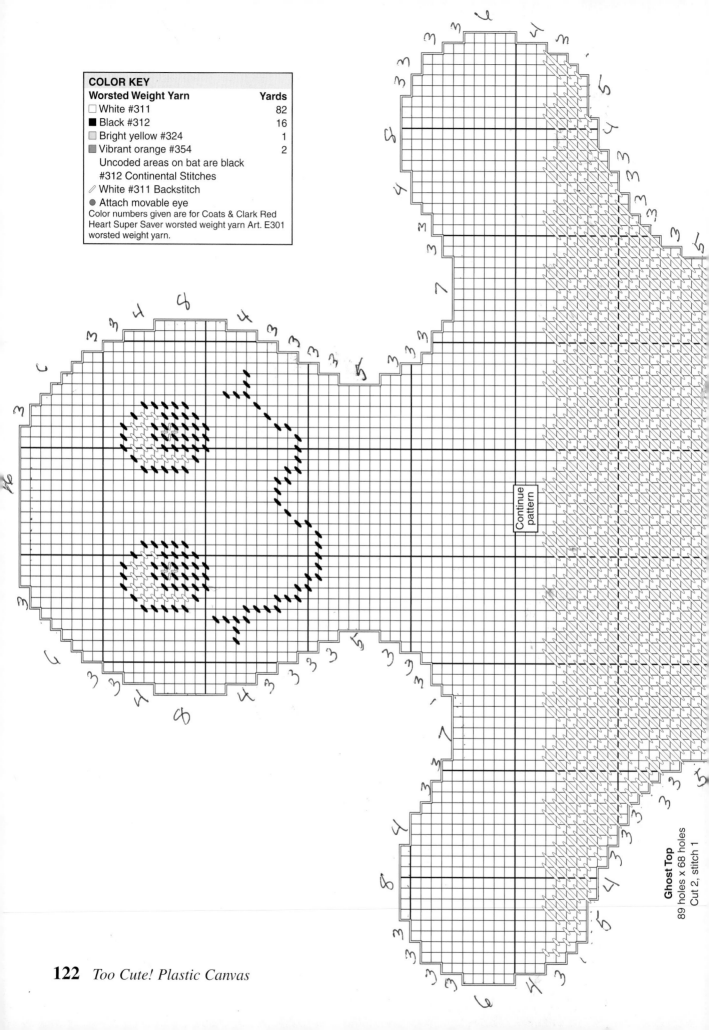

COLOR KEY

Worsted Weight Yarn	Yards
☐ White #311	82
■ Black #312	16
☐ Bright yellow #324	1
■ Vibrant orange #354	2

Uncoded areas on bat are black
#312 Continental Stitches

✐ White #311 Backstitch

● Attach movable eye

Color numbers given are for Coats & Clark Red Heart Super Saver worsted weight yarn Art. E301 worsted weight yarn.

Continue pattern

Ghost Top
89 holes x 68 holes
Cut 2, stitch 1

Ghost Bottom
63 holes x 88 holes
Cut 2, stitch 1

Continue pattern

Goofy Ghouls Magnet Trio

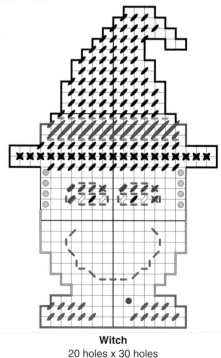

Skill Level

Beginner

Size

Monster: 2½ inches W x 3⅛ inches H
Mummy: 2½ inches W x 3¼ inches H
Witch: 3⅛ inches W x 4⅝ inches H

"Liven up" your Halloween party with this trio of not-so-spooky ghoul magnets!

Designs by
Susan Leinberger

Materials

- ½ sheet 7-count plastic canvas
- Uniek Needloft plastic canvas yarn as listed in color key
- Uniek Needloft metallic craft cord as listed in color key
- #3 pearl cotton as listed in color key
- #16 tapestry needle
- ½-inch pompoms: 1 bright green, 2 lime green
- 7 inches adhesive-backed magnet strips
- Hot-glue gun

Instructions

1. Cut plastic canvas according to graphs.

2. Stitch and Overcast monster and mummy, working uncoded area on monster with bright green Continental Stitches and uncoded area on mummy with bright yellow Continental Stitches. Use a double strand to work monster's hair. Work solid silver Backstitches for bolts in monster while Overcasting.

3. Stitch and Overcast witch, working uncoded area with bright green Continental Stitches. Do not Overcast area adjacent to gray Lark's Head Knots.

4. When background stitching is completed, Backstitch eyes, eyebrows and mouth with black #3 pearl cotton. Backstitch hatband with bright orange yarn. With holly yarn, work French Knot wart on witch's chin, wrapping yarn around needle two times.

5. Using gray, work four Lark's Head Knots on each side for hair where indicated on witch, clipping each strand of hair about 2½ inches long. Use needle to separate plies of yarn and "fluff" hair.

COLOR KEY	
Plastic Canvas Yarn	**Yards**
■ Black #00	5
■ Holly #27	1
□ Eggshell #39	3
□ White #41	1
■ Bright purple #64	2
Uncoded areas on monster and witch are bright green #61 Continental Stitches	5
Uncoded area on mummy is bright yellow #63 Continental Stitches	
⁄ Bright green #61 Overcasting	
⁄ Bright orange #58 Backstitch	1
● Holly #27 French Knot	
○ Gray #38 Lark's Head Knot	2
Metallic Craft Cord	
⁄ Solid silver #21 Backstitch and Overcasting	1
#3 Pearl Cotton	
⁄ Black #403 Backstitch	4
Color numbers given are for Uniek Needloft plastic canvas yarn and metallic craft cord.	

Witch
20 holes x 30 holes
Cut 1

6. For noses, glue lime green pompoms to mummy and witch; glue bright green pompom to monster.

7. Cut magnet strips into three pieces and affix one to wrong side of each ghoul. ✂

Sunflower Season Caddy & Candyholder

Continued from page 118

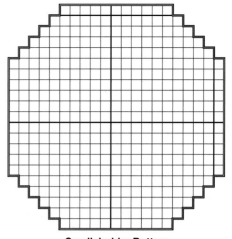

Candleholder Bottom
21 holes x 21 holes
Cut 1 from clear
Do not stitch

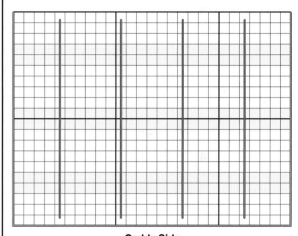

Caddy Side
27 holes x 20 holes
Cut 2 from orange

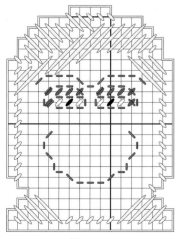

Mummy
16 holes x 21 holes
Cut 1

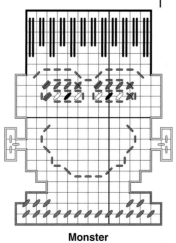

Monster
16 holes x 20 holes
Cut 1

Spooky Doorknob Hanger

Skill Level
Beginner

Size
4⅝ inches W x 9½ inches H

Materials
- 1 sheet 7-count plastic canvas
- Worsted weight yarn as listed in color key
- #16 tapestry needle
- 10 (7mm) round movable eyes
- Hot-glue gun

Instructions

1. Cut plastic canvas according to graphs.

2. Stitch pieces following graphs, working uncoded areas on door with light brown Continental Stitches. Leave red and blue bars on haunted house unstitched for shutter and door attachments.

3. When background stitching is completed, add white French Knot doorknob to door.

4. Overcast house; Overcast top, bottom and right edges of door; Overcast top, bottom and one side edge of each shutter.

5. Using light brown, Whipstitch unstitched edge of door to house where indicated with blue line. Using dark green, Whipstitch unstitched edges of shutters to windows where indicated with red lines, placing small shutters at top window and large shutters at all other windows.

6. Using photo as a guide, glue two eyes in each window, and two to ghost in doorway. ✂

Five pairs of unblinking eyes will send shivers up your spine as you hang this eerie door hanger on Halloween night!

Design by
Patricia Klesh

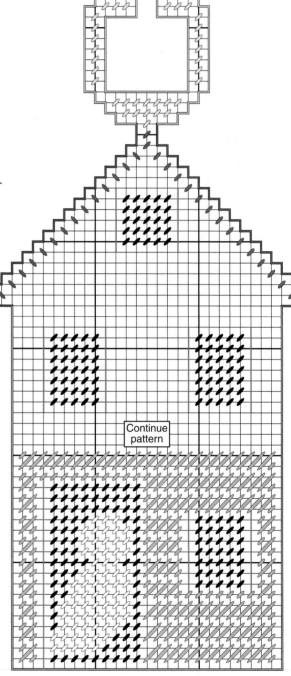

House
30 holes x 63 holes
Cut 1

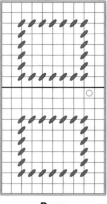

Door
10 holes x 18 holes
Cut 1

Large Shutter
3 holes x 8 holes
Cut 6

Small Shutter
3 holes x 6 holes
Cut 2

Halloween Heads Party Favors

Skill Level
Beginner

Size

Each box:
2¾-inches square

Ghost: 3⅝ inches W x 3¾ inches H

Ghoul: 4½ inches W x 3¾ inches H

Pumpkin: 3⅞ inches W x 3¾ inches H

Witch: 4¼ inches W x 4 inches H

A ghost, a ghoul, a witch and a pumpkin offer four fun ways to say, "Happy Halloween!"

Designs by Joyce Livingston

Materials

- ⅔ sheet clear 7-count plastic canvas
- ¼ vertical sheet each 7-count plastic canvas: orange, white, bright purple and bright green
- Uniek Needloft plastic canvas yarn as listed in color key
- 6-strand embroidery floss as listed in color key
- #16 tapestry needle
- 8 (11mm) movable eyes
- Black thread or floss
- Tacky craft glue

Instructions

1. Cut one each of ghost, ghoul, pumpkin and witch from clear plastic canvas according to graphs.

2. Cut five 17-hole x 17-hole pieces each from orange, white, bright purple and bright green plastic canvas for box sides and bottoms.

3. Stitch and Overcast heads following graphs. When background stitching is completed, work black floss Backstitches for mouths. Using photo as a guide, glue eyes to heads.

4. For each box, matching colors of yarn and plastic canvas, Whipstitch sides together, then Whipstitch sides to bottom. If desired, Overcast top edges.

5. Matching color of face to color of box, center and glue head to one side of each box, making sure bottom edges are even. ✂

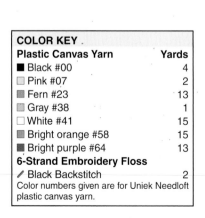

```
COLOR KEY
Plastic Canvas Yarn                    Yards
■ Black #00                               4
□ Pink #07                                2
■ Fern #23                               13
■ Gray #38                                1
□ White #41                              15
■ Bright orange #58                      15
■ Bright purple #64                      13
6-Strand Embroidery Floss
✎ Black Backstitch                        2
Color numbers given are for Uniek Needloft
plastic canvas yarn.
```

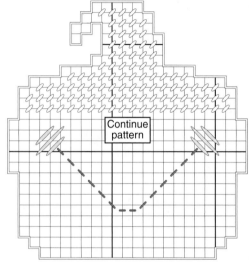

Ghost Head
23 holes x 24 holes
Cut 1 from clear

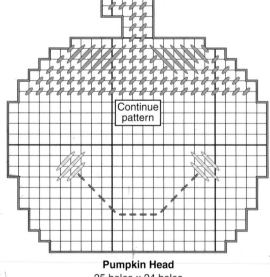

Pumpkin Head
25 holes x 24 holes
Cut 1 from clear

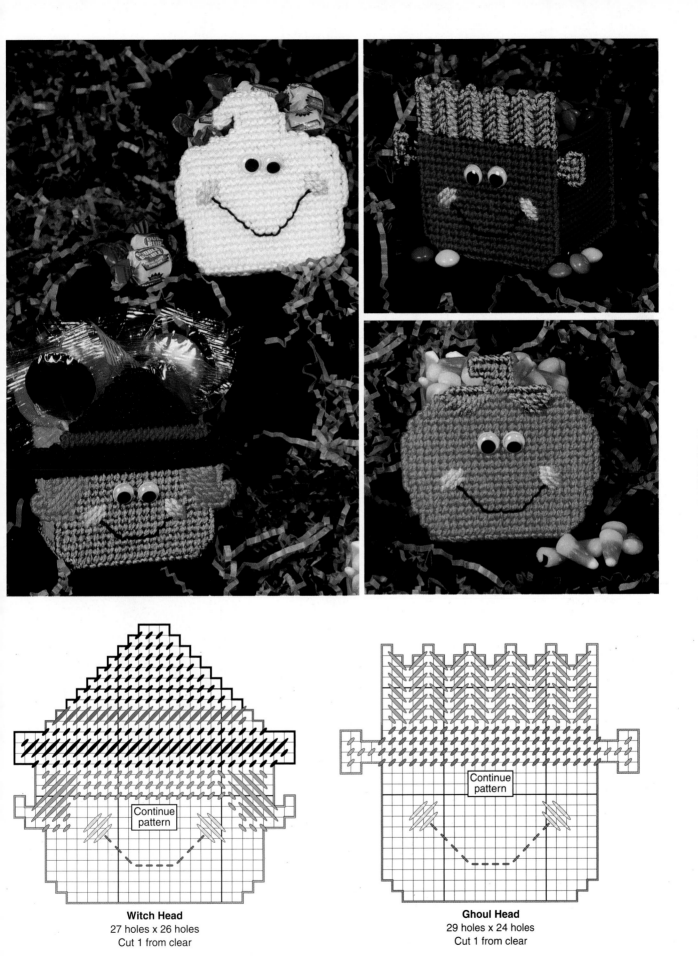

Witch Head
27 holes x 26 holes
Cut 1 from clear

Ghoul Head
29 holes x 24 holes
Cut 1 from clear

Continue pattern

Continue pattern

"Franklin" stein

**Have a little
"ghoul"
with your
goulash!
This friendly
Frankenstein
puts on
his best
Halloween
face to
haunt your
table!**

Design by
Debra Arch

Materials
- 3 sheets clear 7-count plastic canvas
- Small amount black 7-count plastic canvas
- 4½-inch plastic canvas radial circle
- Coats & Clark Red Heart Super Saver worsted weight yarn Art. E301 as listed in color key
- Coats & Clark Red Heart Kids worsted weight yarn Art. E711 as listed in color key
- #16 tapestry needle
- 10½-inch tall empty, clean potato chip canister
- Sand (optional)
- 1 gallon zip-tight plastic bag (optional)
- Hot-glue gun

Cutting
1. Cut sutures from black plastic canvas (page 132), cutting away blue lines. Cut head top from plastic canvas radial circle (page 131), cutting away gray area.

2. Cut body, jacket, arms, hands and shoes from clear plastic canvas (pages 131, 132 and 133).

Jacket & Arms
1. Stitch right side of jacket with light gray Continental Stitches, leaving blue shaded areas unworked. Turn jacket over and stitch light gray Reverse Continental Stitches in blue shaded areas (lapels).

2. Using light gray through step 4, Overcast

bottom, front and neckline edges from B to C. Fold jacket so wrong sides are facing, placing points B together and points C together.

3. Beginning at point A on left side of jacket, Whipstitch edges together to points B, forming shoulder and sleeve seam. Repeat with right side, Whipstitching from point A to points C.

4. To make inside sleeve seam, press front against back and work light gray Backstitches and Running Stitches where indicated through both thicknesses.

5. Stitching over these light gray stitches, work a long black Straight Stitch from back to front at top of stitch, around bottom edge and back to starting point; tie a small tight knot in back and clip short.

6. Fold down lapel areas and tack to front of jacket with light gray (see photo).

7. Stitch hand bottom pieces. For hand on each arm, stitch bottom five bars of arm only, leaving remaining area unworked. Whipstitch long side edges together, then Whipstitch one hand bottom to bottom edge. Top edges will remain unstitched.

8. Placing seam at the back, insert one arm into each sleeve, allowing lime stitches to show as in photo.

Body

1. Stitch body following graph, using two strands black for hair as indicated.

2. When background Stitching is completed, use orange to work Backstitches on front of shirt and Straight Stitches for cheeks. Work mouth and eyes with black.

3. Whipstitch side edges together with adjacent colors, forming a tube; Overcast bottom edge.

Head Top & Shoes

1. Using two strands black, work stitches on head top from center to outside row of holes, filling in with shorter stitches as shown.

2. Stitch shoes top only, leaving bottom piece unworked. Whipstitch top and bottom pieces together.

Assembly

1. Using two strands black yarn, Whipstitch head top to top edge of body. For "flat top," while Whipstitching forehead area (green stitches), wrap yarn around your thumb to form a loop, then do a regular Whipstitch in same place to lock in loop before going on to next hole.

2. If weight is desired, place sand in plastic bag; seal shut. Roll up bag and insert in potato chip canister. Glue lid securely in place.

3. Insert canister in body tube. Glue shoes to bottom of body. Using photo as a guide throughout, wrap jacket around body; glue in place. Glue sutures to face. ✂

COLOR KEY

Worsted Weight Yarn	Yards
☐ Orange #245	30
■ Black #312	125
☐ Light gray #341	60
☐ Lime #2652	20
╱ Orange #245 Backstitch and Straight Stitch	
╱ Black #312 Backstitch and Straight Stitch	
╱ Light gray #341 Backstitch and Running Stitch	
● Black #312 French Knot	

Color numbers given are for Coats & Clark Red Heart Super Saver worsted weight yarn Art. E301 and Kids worsted weight yarn Art. E711.

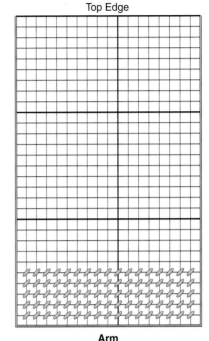

Top Edge

Arm
18 holes x 29 holes
Cut 2 from clear
Do not stitch uncoded area

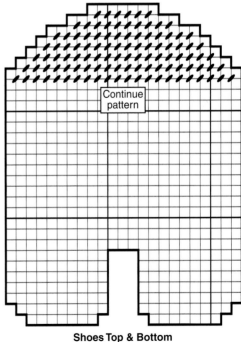

Head Top
Cut 1 from radial circle,
cutting away gray area
Stitch with a double strand

Continue pattern

Shoes Top & Bottom
23 holes x 30 holes
Cut 2 from clear, stitch 1

Continue pattern

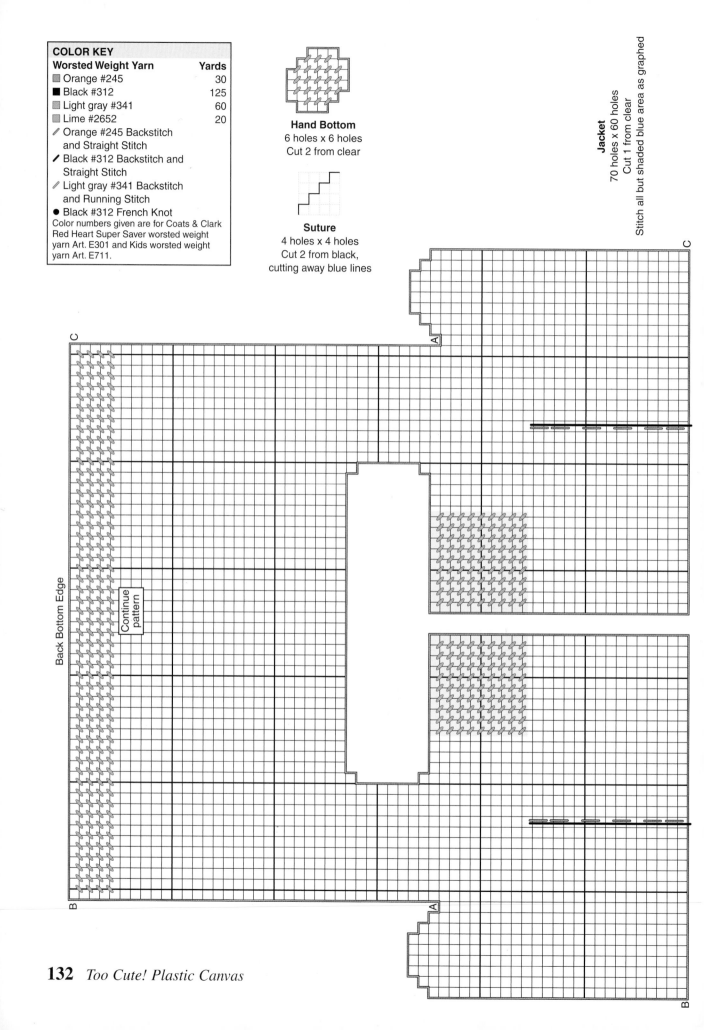

COLOR KEY

Worsted Weight Yarn	Yards
■ Orange #245	30
■ Black #312	125
■ Light gray #341	60
■ Lime #2652	20

/ Orange #245 Backstitch
  and Straight Stitch

/ Black #312 Backstitch and
  Straight Stitch

/ Light gray #341 Backstitch
  and Running Stitch

● Black #312 French Knot

Color numbers given are for Coats & Clark
Red Heart Super Saver worsted weight
yarn Art. E301 and Kids worsted weight
yarn Art. E711.

Hand Bottom
6 holes x 6 holes
Cut 2 from clear

Suture
4 holes x 4 holes
Cut 2 from black,
cutting away blue lines

Jacket
70 holes x 60 holes
Cut 1 from clear
Stitch all but shaded blue area as graphed

Back Bottom Edge

Continue pattern

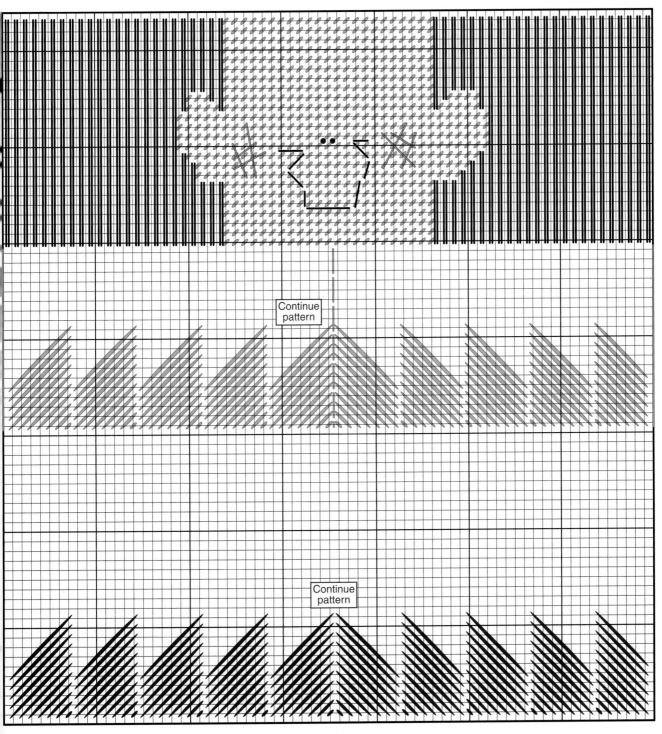

Body
70 holes x 74 holes
Cut 1 from clear

Haunted House Tissue Topper

Skill Level
Intermediate

Size
Fits boutique-style tissue box

This irresistible tissue cover will spook you silly—it's haunted by friendly ghosts and smiling pumpkins!

Design by
Nancy Dorman

Materials
- 2 sheets 10-count plastic canvas
- Sport weight yarn as listed in color key
- 6-strand embroidery floss as listed in color key
- #18 tapestry needle
- Orange pumpkin confetti
- Autumn leaf pick with variegated colors
- Hot-glue gun

Instructions
1. Cut plastic canvas according to graphs (pages 135 and 143).

2. Stitch and Overcast shutters. Stitch remaining pieces, working uncoded areas with black yarn Continental Stitches.

3. When background stitching is completed, work tree branches with light brown yarn. Using embroidery floss, work black Backstitches and French Knots. Work cobwebs in corners of windows and doors with 1 ply light gray.

4. Overcast inside edge of top and bottom edges of sides. Using Binding Stitch or regular Whipstitch, Whipstitch sides together, then Whipstitch sides to top.

5. Tack shutters next to windows with dark gray yarn, allowing some to "hang" crooked.

6. Glue pumpkin confetti to all windows except the turret window, and one pumpkin to each corner on top. Cut tiny leaves from pick and glue as desired to branches and roofs. ✂

Materials

- 1 artist-size sheet 7-count plastic canvas
- Coats & Clark Red Heart Kids worsted weight yarn Art. E711 as listed in color key
- #16 tapestry needle
- 4 inches ⅝-inch wide hook-and-loop tape
- Glue or hand-sewing needle and matching sewing thread

Instructions

1. Align red lines on the two graphs (this page and page 143), then cut as one piece from artist-size plastic canvas, cutting one 150-hole x 35-hole piece.

2. Stitch piece following graph, working uncoded areas with yellow Continental Stitches. Overcast flames with orange, band with yellow and candles with adjacent colors.

3. When background stitching is completed, work orange Straight Stitch on each flame. Embroider lettering with blue.

4. Cut hook-and-loop tape into 2-inch lengths. Using glue or hand-sewing needle and sewing thread, adhere the two loop pieces to wrong side on one end of band; adhere hook pieces to right side on other end of band. ✂

Graphs continued on page 143

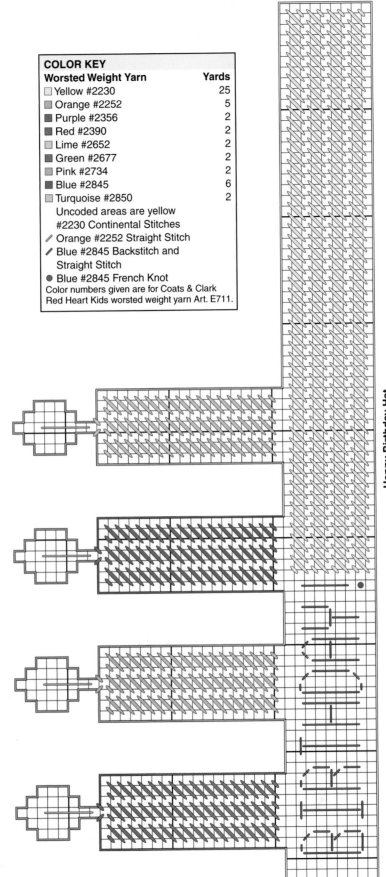

COLOR KEY

Worsted Weight Yarn	Yards
☐ Yellow #2230	25
☐ Orange #2252	5
■ Purple #2356	2
■ Red #2390	2
☐ Lime #2652	2
■ Green #2677	2
☐ Pink #2734	2
■ Blue #2845	6
☐ Turquoise #2850	2

Uncoded areas are yellow #2230 Continental Stitches
⟋ Orange #2252 Straight Stitch
⟋ Blue #2845 Backstitch and Straight Stitch
● Blue #2845 French Knot

Color numbers given are for Coats & Clark Red Heart Kids worsted weight yarn Art. E711.

Happy Birthday Hat
Align red line on this graph with red line on left part of graph and cut as one

Harvest Bear Tissue Topper

Skill Level

Beginner

Size

Fits boutique-style tissue box

This adorable bear cub will put all your Thanksgiving guests in the spirit of sharing!

Materials

- 1½ sheets 7-count plastic canvas
- Uniek Needloft plastic canvas yarn as listed in color key
- #16 tapestry needle

Instructions

1. Cut plastic canvas according to graphs (page 140).

2. Stitch pieces following graphs, working uncoded areas with forest Continental Stitches. Work yellow Backstitches when background stitching is completed.

3. Using forest throughout, Overcast bottom edges of sides and inside edges of top. Whipstitch sides together, then Whipstitch sides to top. ✂

Graphs continued on page 140

Graphs continued on page 140

COLOR KEY	
Plastic Canvas Yarn	**Yards**
■ Black #00	2
■ Cinnamon #14	6
☐ Christmas green #28	8
☐ Beige #40	10
☐ Camel #43	17
■ Bittersweet #52	8
■ Turquoise #54	6
Uncoded areas are forest #29 Continental Stitches	32
✎ Forest #29 Overcasting and Whipstitching	
✎ Yellow #57 Backstitch	8
Color numbers given are for Uniek Needloft plastic canvas yarn.	

Design by
Angie Arickx

Kiss the Cook

Skill Level
Beginner

Size
5⅜ inches W x
5⅛ inches H

Add a
fun touch
of Early
American
charm to
your kitchen
with this
sweet
Pilgrim
ornament!

Materials
- ¼ sheet 7-count plastic canvas
- Uniek Needloft plastic canvas yarn as listed in color key
- #5 pearl cotton as listed in color key
- Kreinik ⅛-inch metallic ribbon as listed in color key
- #16 tapestry needle

Instructions

1. Cut plastic canvas according to graph (page 140).

2. Stitch and Overcast piece, working uncoded areas on pilgrims with cinnamon Continental Stitches and uncoded area on sign with eggshell Continental Stitches.

3. Using eggshell, add small Straight Stitches to form icing drops to cake in girl's hands.

4. Using gold metallic ribbon, Backstitch buckle on boy's hat.

5. Using black #5 pearl cotton throughout, Backstitch and Straight Stitch words and remaining details, passing over each eye twice. Add French Knot to letter "i," wrapping pearl cotton around needle once.

6. Using burgundy throughout, add French Knot "cherries" to base of turkey, wrapping yarn around needle once; add French Knot "cherry" to top of cake, wrapping yarn around needle twice.

7. Secure a length of gold metallic ribbon through back of stitching at top of one hat; secure remaining end to back of other hat, allowing loop to extend 2½ inches above ornament, cutting excess. ✂

Design by
Janelle Giese

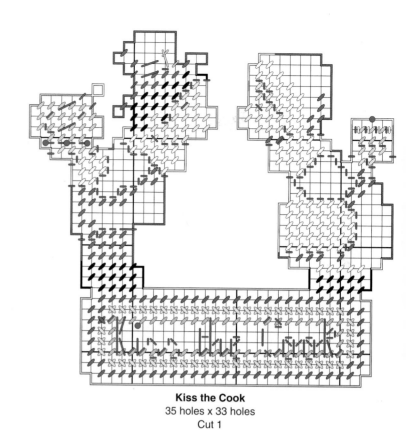

Kiss the Cook
35 holes x 33 holes
Cut 1

Harvest Bear Tissue Topper

Continued from page 138

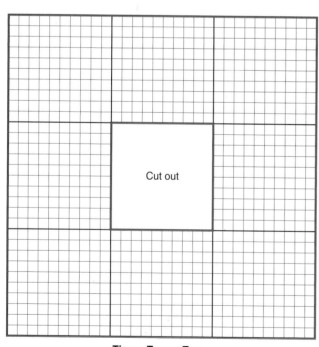

Tissue Topper Top
30 holes x 30 holes
Cut 1

Cut out

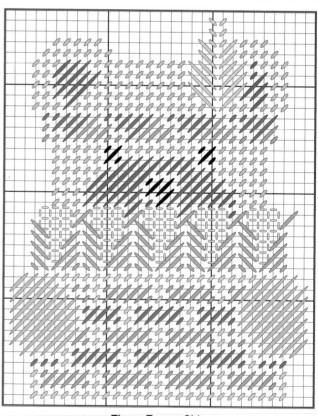

Tissue Topper Side
30 holes x 37 holes
Cut 4

Turkey Farmer Wall Hanging

Materials

- 1 sheet 7-count plastic canvas
- Uniek Needloft plastic canvas yarn as listed in color key
- #16 tapestry needle
- 2 (6mm) round black beads
- 2 (½-inch) red buttons
- ¾-inch metal or plastic ring
- 3-inch straw doll hat
- Hand-sewing needle
- Black thread or floss
- Tacky craft glue

Instructions

1. Cut plastic canvas according to graphs (page 142).

2. Stitch and Overcast pieces following graphs, working uncoded areas on turkey with white Continental Stitches. *Note: Uncoded portion on tail should remain unstitched.*

3. Work maple Backstitches on tail when background stitching is completed. Using 1-ply tangerine, sew buttons to turkey where indicated on graph. Using maple, Whipstitch ring to top edge of tail where indicated on graph.

4. Use photo as a guide through step 6. With hand-sewing needle and black thread or floss, sew black beads to head for eyes where indicated on graph. Center and glue beak/ wattle to head below eyes; allow to dry.

5. Glue wings to back of body and tail to back of wings, allowing each to dry before proceeding.

6. Cut brim from back half of hat; seal edges with glue. Glue hat to head. ✂

Skill Level
Beginner

Size
6¾ inches W x
12 inches H

Your friends will love this jovial turkey—he's a real "tom" boy!

Design by
Nancy Marshall

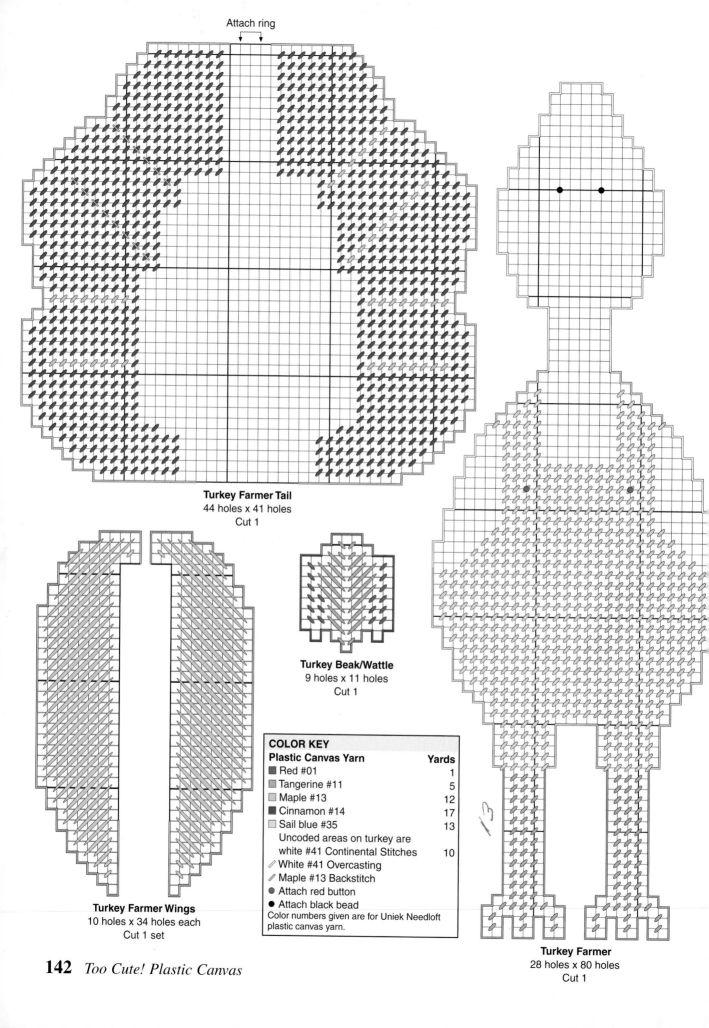

Attach ring

Turkey Farmer Tail
44 holes x 41 holes
Cut 1

Turkey Beak/Wattle
9 holes x 11 holes
Cut 1

Turkey Farmer Wings
10 holes x 34 holes each
Cut 1 set

COLOR KEY

Plastic Canvas Yarn	Yards
■ Red #01	1
▨ Tangerine #11	5
▨ Maple #13	12
■ Cinnamon #14	17
▢ Sail blue #35	13
Uncoded areas on turkey are white #41 Continental Stitches	10
⁄ White #41 Overcasting	
⁄ Maple #13 Backstitch	
● Attach red button	
● Attach black bead	

Color numbers given are for Uniek Needloft
plastic canvas yarn.

Turkey Farmer
28 holes x 80 holes
Cut 1

Assembly

1. Use 12 strands floss to attach buttons with Cross Stitches to snowman in unworked areas, using very light beauty rose for top button and medium spring green for bottom button.

2. Place banner on frame; Whipstitch outside edges together with medium spring green.

3. Glue sign to unworked area on banner.

4. For rope, cut a 12-inch 6-ply length of medium wheat. Thread one end of length from front to back through hole indicated on mitten on left side, leaving about a ⅝-inch tail on front. Secure floss on backside, then thread through same hole to front.

5. Leaving slack as shown in photo, thread yarn from front to back through bottom hole indicated on right mitten, then from back to front through hole indicated just above insertion point. Bring floss back down through hole on right side of right mitten, anchor on backside, then thread to front through same hole, leaving a ⅝-inch tail.

6. Glue stars and heart to rope and banner.

7. Glue rickrack around edge on backside of assembled banner. Center banner on felt backing and glue in place.

8. Fold each tab in half; glue ends together, making a loop. Glue tabs to top backside of felt about 1 inch from each side edge. Insert twig through tabs to hang banner. ✂

Banner Heart
7 holes x 7 holes
Cut 1

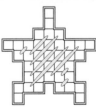

Banner Star
9 holes x 9 holes
Cut 2

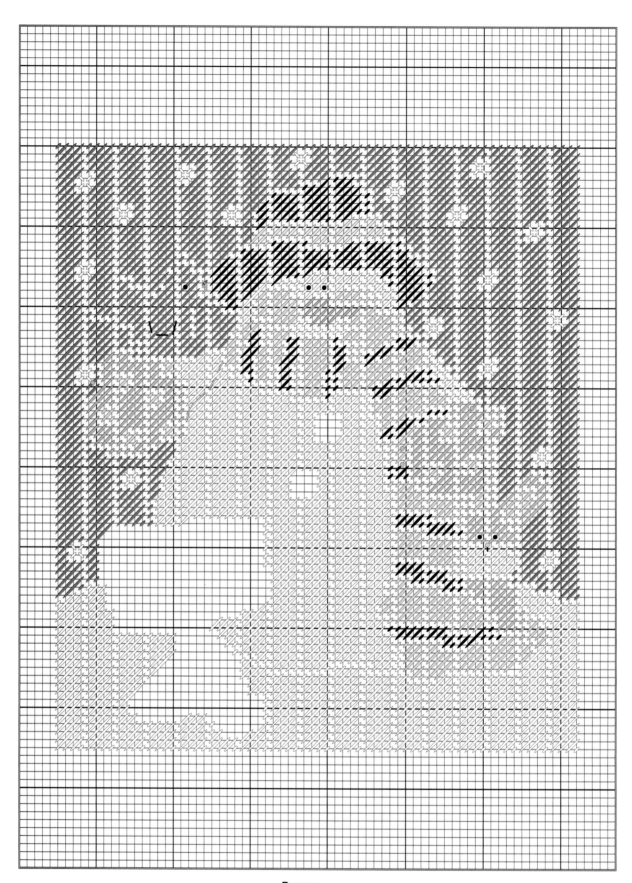

Banner
77 holes x 105 holes
Cut 1

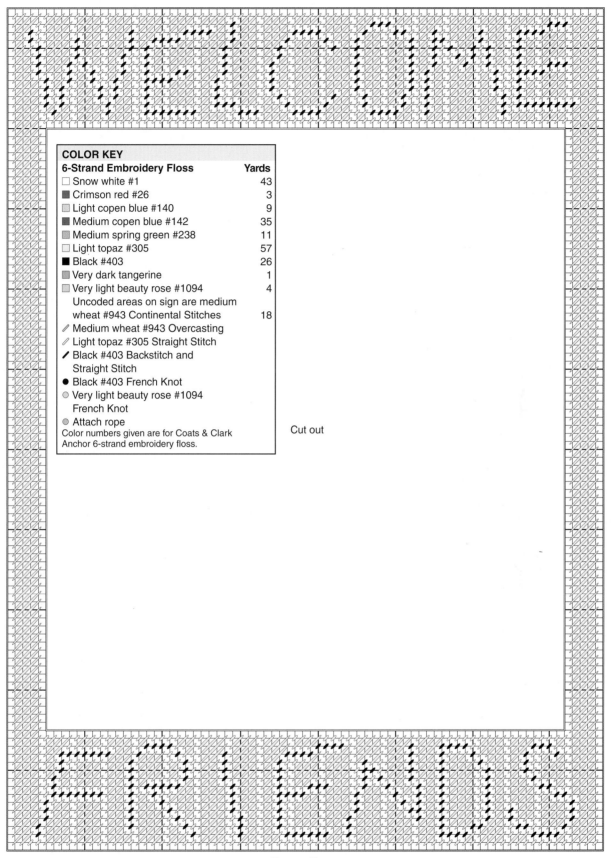

COLOR KEY

6-Strand Embroidery Floss	Yards
☐ Snow white #1	43
■ Crimson red #26	3
▨ Light copen blue #140	9
■ Medium copen blue #142	35
▨ Medium spring green #238	11
☐ Light topaz #305	57
■ Black #403	26
▨ Very dark tangerine	1
☐ Very light beauty rose #1094	4
Uncoded areas on sign are medium wheat #943 Continental Stitches	18

⟋ Medium wheat #943 Overcasting
⟋ Light topaz #305 Straight Stitch
╱ Black #403 Backstitch and Straight Stitch
● Black #403 French Knot
○ Very light beauty rose #1094 French Knot
○ Attach rope

Color numbers given are for Coats & Clark Anchor 6-strand embroidery floss.

Cut out

Banner Frame
77 holes x 105 holes
Cut 1

Cinnamon Stick Snowman & Santa

Skill Level
Intermediate

Size
Snowman: 5 inches W x 5⅜ inches H

Santa: 4⅛ inches W x 5⅝ inches H

Add freshness and spice to your kitchen this season with this sweet, delightful duo!

Designs by Kathy Wirth

Materials
- ½ sheet 10-count plastic canvas
- Coats & Clark Anchor 6-strand embroidery floss as listed in color key
- #22 tapestry needle
- ⁷/₁₆-inch black button
- 4 (⅜-inch) gold jingle bells
- 12 inches 24-gauge gold wire
- 5 (3-inch) cinnamon sticks
- 10mm red glitter pompom
- Wire cutters
- Pencil
- Fishing line
- Craft knife
- Fabric glue
- Hot-glue gun

Project Notes
Unless otherwise instructed, stitch with two strands (12-plies) floss.

Keep stitches flat and untwisted by smoothing over finger while stitching.

When gluing, use hot glue unless otherwise instructed.

COLOR KEY	
6-Strand Embroidery Floss	**Yards**
☐ Snow white #1	43
◼ Medium dark burgundy #20 and crimson red #26	7 each
◼ Crimson red #26	
◼ Medium spring green #238	11
☐ Medium jonquil #297	12
◼ Black #403	12
☐ Very light flesh #1011	1
☐ Very light beauty rose #1094	1
Uncoded areas are snow white #1 Continental Stitches	
╱ Black #403 Backstitch Straight Stitch	
○ Medium jonquil #297 Lark's Head Knot	
● Black #403 French Knot	
● Attach shoe bow	
○ Attach wire	
○ Attach hanger	
Color numbers given are for Coats & Clark Anchor 6-strand embroidery floss.	

Instructions
1. Cut plastic canvas according to graphs (this page and page 154).

2. Stitch pieces following graphs, working uncoded areas on sign, Santa and snowman's face with white Continental Stitches and combining one strand (6 plies) each crimson red and medium dark burgundy to work Santa's suit and snowman's scarf.

3. When background stitching is completed, use 6 strands black floss to work letters on sign, snowman's mouth and eyes, Santa's eyes and flecks in Santa's fur trim.

4. Overcast Santa, sign and mitten, leaving edges between arrows on left side and between blue dots on right side of mitten unworked. Overcast snowman, leaving edges of unstitched mitten unworked.

5. Using 6 strands medium jonquil throughout, for fringe on snowman's scarf, work each Lark's Head Knot where indicated, cutting ends to about ½-inch-long. Thread a length of floss through hole indicated on each of Santa's boots; tie in bows.

Finishing
1. Use 12 strands crimson red to attach button to center of snowman's vest, threading floss from back to front through two holes on button; tie knot on front of button and trim ends.

2. Matching left edges, Whipstitch left side of mitten to left mitten edge on snowman from

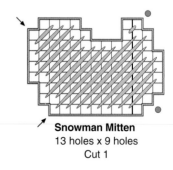

Snowman Mitten
13 holes x 9 holes
Cut 1

arrow to arrow. Whipstitch right edge of mitten from dot to dot to bars highlighted with green.

3. Cut about ¾ inch off one cinnamon stick; glue ¾-inch piece to one end of another cinnamon stick to make it longer. Glue sign to lengthened stick, covering joined area. Insert stick in mitten; glue in place (see photo).

4. Hot-glue remaining three full-length sticks to back of Santa's bag, allowing 1¼ inches to extend above bag.

5. Using wire cutters, cut wire into two 6-inch lengths. Curl each length by wrapping unevenly around pencil. Thread two bells onto each wire (see photo), wrapping wire through loops in bells; glue to secure.

6. For each ornament, insert wire into canvas under thumb on right side; glue

wire end to backside. Glue bottom bell to front.

7. Use fabric glue to attach pompom to Santa's hat; add glue to all knots in button and in bows, and to fringe on back of snowman.

8. For hangers, thread desired length of fishing line through holes indicated. Ties ends together in a knot to form a loop for hanging. ✂

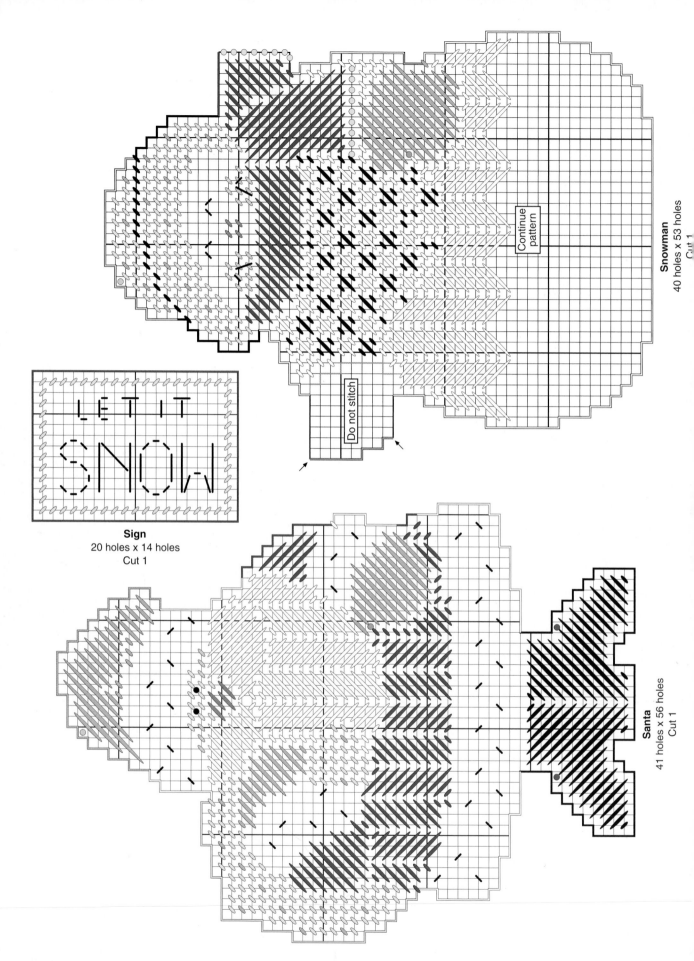

Snowman
40 holes x 53 holes
Cut 1

Continue pattern

Do not stitch

Sign
20 holes x 14 holes
Cut 1

Santa
41 holes x 56 holes
Cut 1

Prancer

Skill Level
Intermediate

Size
7¼ inches W x
11¼inches H

Festive and
fun, this
adorable
reindeer
will perk up
your table
or mantel
with holiday
cheer!

Design by
Debra Arch

Materials

- 2 sheets clear 7-count plastic canvas
- 6-inch plastic canvas radial circle
- 2 (4½-inch) plastic canvas radial circles
- Coats & Clark Red Heart Super Saver worsted weight yarn Art. E300 as listed in color key
- #16 tapestry needle
- 10½-inch-tall empty, clean potato chip canister
- Approximately 20 inches 22-gauge wire
- 2 (12mm) round black wooden beads
- 19mm silver jingle bell
- 4-inch red metallic ribbon bow
- 25 inches green garland
- Approximately 45 inches silver tinsel garland
- Approximately 45 inches red bead garland
- Black permanent marker
- Small amount fiberfill
- Hot-glue gun

Cutting & Stitching

1. Cut plastic canvas according to graphs, cutting away gray area from 4½-inch radial circles.

2. For antlers, cut away inside area of 6-inch radial circle, leaving the first outermost row of holes, then cut through this row at one point so it is no longer connected.

3. Cut off top 1½ inches from potato chip canister. Glue lid back on; set aside.

4. Weave 22-gauge wire through every fifth hole of antlers to add strength and flexibility, leaving about 3-inches of wire extending from each end. Overcast antler edges with black yarn, then work a running stitch down center to fill in. Use black marker to color plastic canvas still showing.

5. Stitch remaining pieces following graphs, working stitches on head top from center to outside row of holes, filling in with shorter stitches as shown.

6. For body, Whipstitch top 3 inches of side edges together, leaving remainder temporarily unstitched. Set aside.

7. Whipstitch wrong sides of head pieces together, attaching jingle bell to tip of nose while Whipstitching and inserting small amount of fiberfill in nose area before closing.

8. For each leg, Whipstitch wrong sides of two leg pieces together around side and top edges, then Whipstitch hoof bottom to bottom edges of leg.

Assembly

1. Using heather taupe, Whipstitch head top to top edge of body. With body seam at back, align top edge of head across center of head top; stitch in place.

2. To fasten head to body, using black yarn, attach beads to head front for eyes, bringing yarn completely through to wrong side of body front.

3. Using photo as a guide, bend antlers into desired shape. Thread wire ends of antler through center of head top behind top edge of face; twist wire ends together to secure.

4. Using heather taupe, finish Whipstitching side edges of body together, completing back seam. Slip body over potato chip canister; Whipstitch unstitched bottom to bottom edge of reindeer.

5. Wrap green garland under reindeer chin and up around front of antlers at top of head. Twist ends together, forming a wreath. Wrap silver tinsel garland, then red bead garland around wreath, cutting off any excess. Glue wreath to top of head. Attach red bow to wreath as desired.

6. For hair tuft, wrap a length of heather taupe around four fingers 15 times. Remove from fingers and tie in center; cut loops. Glue to top of head in front of wreath.

7. Place tops of legs up under wreath and glue to body. Glue wreath to legs. ✄

Hoof Bottom
7 holes x 5 holes
Cut 2

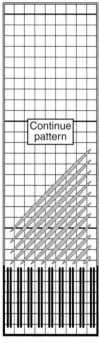

Leg
9 holes x 31 holes
Cut 2

COLOR KEY	
Worsted Weight Yarn	**Yards**
■ Black #312	15
☐ Heather taupe #403	125
● Attach black bead	

Color numbers given are for Coats & Clark Red Heart Super Saver worsted weight yarn Art. E300.

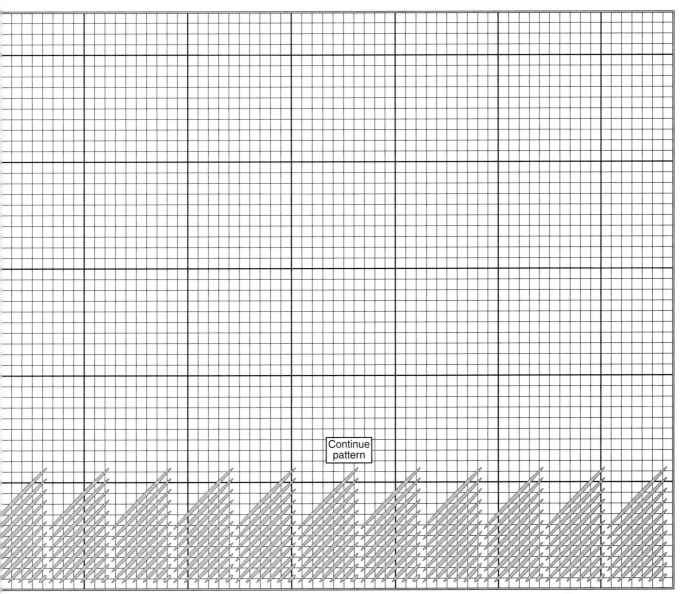

Body
67 holes x 54 holes
Cut 1

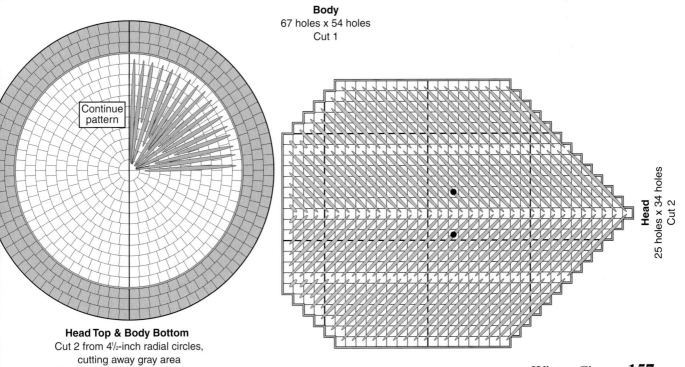

Head Top & Body Bottom
Cut 2 from 4½-inch radial circles,
cutting away gray area
Stitch 1 as graphed for head top
Do not stitch body bottom

Head
25 holes x 34 holes
Cut 2

Happy Elf Door Hanger

Materials

- 1 sheet 7-count plastic canvas
- Uniek Needloft plastic canvas yarn as listed in color key
- #3 pearl cotton as listed in color key
- #16 tapestry needle
- ½ to 1 yard each four different-color thin ribbons and/or cords

Instructions

1. Cut plastic canvas according to graph.

2. Stitch and Overcast piece, working uncoded areas on shirt and pompom with white Continental Stitches and uncoded areas on bottom gift package and on hat with tangerine Continental Stitches.

3. When background stitching is completed, work pearl cotton embroidery.

4. Attach ribbons and/or cords as desired from back to front on turquoise, watermelon, mermaid and tangerine gift packages, tying bows in front. ✄

COLOR KEY

Plastic Canvas Yarn	Yards
■ Red #01	5
□ Pink #07	8
■ Holly #27	12
□ Mermaid #53	2
□ Turquoise #54	2
■ Watermelon #55	1
Uncoded areas are on gift package and hat are tangerine #11 Continental Stitches	6
Uncoded areas are on shirt and pompom are white #41 Continental Stitches	7
⁄ Tangerine #11 Overcasting	
⁄ White #41 Overcasting	
#3 Pearl Cotton	
✗ Green Cross Stitch	4
● Red French Knot	4
● Dark blue French Knot	1

Color numbers given are for Uniek Needloft plastic canvas yarn.

Skill Level
Beginner

Size
6 inches W x 13½ inches H

This sprightly elf brings good luck and holiday cheer to all who enter!

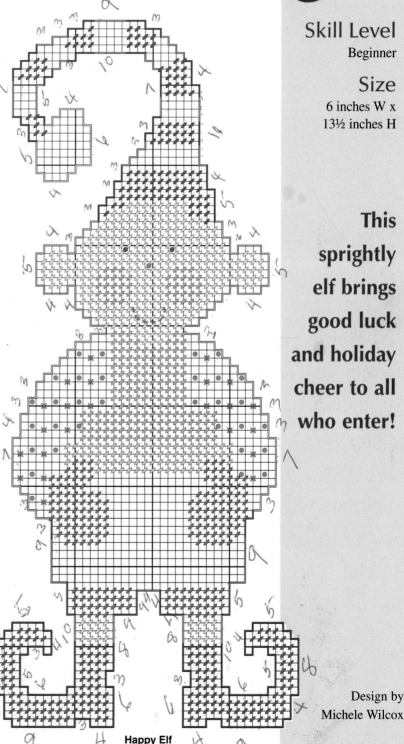

Happy Elf
39 holes x 88 holes
Cut 1

Design by Michele Wilcox

Little Penguin Napkin Ring

Skill Level
Beginner

Size
3½ inches W x
5 inches H x
3 inches D

With his jaunty Santa hat and his cute little scarf, this friendly penguin brings lighthearted cheer to any table!

Design by
Judy Collishaw

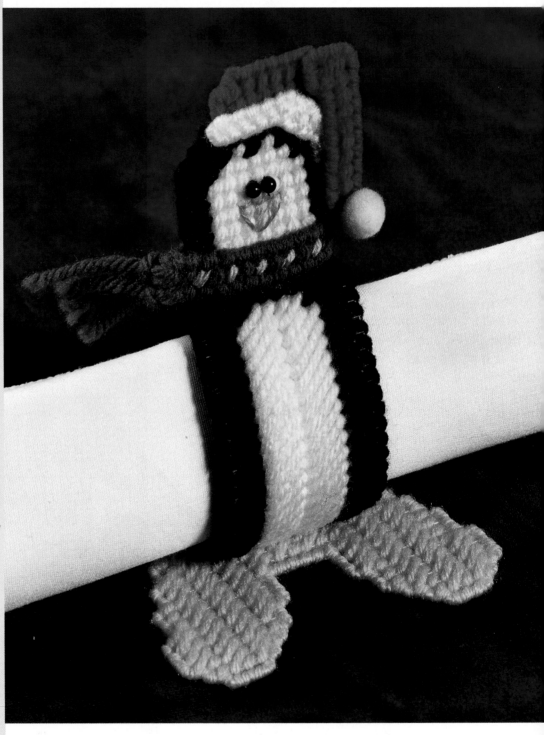

Materials

- ½ sheet 7-count plastic canvas
- Worsted weight yarn as listed in color key
- DMC #5 pearl cotton as listed in color key
- #16 tapestry needle
- ½-inch white pompom
- 2 (4mm) round black beads
- Hand-sewing needle
- Black sewing thread
- Hot-glue gun

Instructions

1. Cut plastic canvas according to graphs.

2. Stitch and Overcast head, feet, hat dangle and hat trim following graphs, working uncoded area on head with white Continental Stitches. Stitch body and scarf as graphed. Whipstitch short edges of each piece together; Overcast remaining edges.

3. When background stitching is completed, work light orange pearl cotton Backstitches on head. Using hand-sewing needle and black thread, sew beads to head where indicated on graph.

4. Cut two 4-inch lengths green yarn and attach to Whipstitched end of scarf with Lark's Head Knots.

5. Fit scarf over top of body (Whipstitched end), placing white tummy in front and scarf fringe to the left; glue wrong side of scarf to side edges of body.

6. Slide head down inside scarf at front of body; glue behind scarf.

7. Glue hat trim to top of head below hat, then glue hat dangle to side edge of hat and head. Glue pompom to end of hat dangle.

8. Center body over back portion of feet and glue in place, making sure to keep body rounded out to hold napkin. ✂

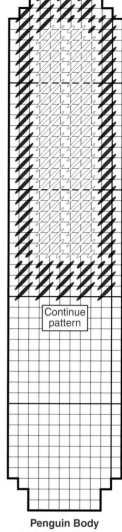

Continue pattern

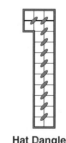

Hat Dangle
3 holes x 11 holes
Cut 1

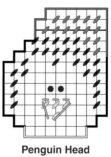

Penguin Head
10 holes x 12 holes
Cut 1

Penguin Body
11 holes x 49 holes
Cut 1

COLOR KEY

Worsted Weight Yarn	Yards
■ Black	7
▨ Yellow	5
□ White	3
■ Green	2
■ Red	1

Uncoded area on head is white Continental Stitches

#5 Pearl Cotton

╱ Tangerine #740 Backstitch	1
● Attach black bead	

Color number given is for DMC #5 pearl cotton.

Hat Trim
8 holes x 5 holes
Cut 1

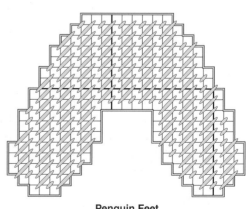

Penquin Feet
23 holes x 17 holes
Cut 1

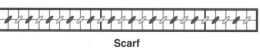

Scarf
25 holes x 2 holes
Cut 1

Tabletop Reindeer

Skill Level

Beginner

Size

Approximately
3¼ inches W x
4⅛ inches L x 6¼
inches H, including
twig legs and antlers

Give your table a rustic look with the woodsy winter charm of these three tiny reindeer!

Materials

Each reindeer

- ⅓ sheet 7-count plastic canvas
- Uniek Needloft plastic canvas yarn as listed in color key
- #16 tapestry needle
- 1 (1¾-inch-long x ¹⁄₁₆-inch in diameter) twig (for neck)
- 2 (2- to 2½-inch-long x ¹⁄₁₆-inch in diameter) twigs with shoots (for antlers)
- 4 (2¾-inch-long x ¹⁄₁₆-inch in diameter) twigs (for legs)
- Hot-glue gun
- Paintbrush
- Brown acrylic paint

Project Note

Materials list, instructions and yardage are for one reindeer.

Instructions

1. Paint all twigs brown and set aside to dry.

2. Cut and stitch plastic canvas according to graphs.

3. Overcast inside and outside edges of body; Overcast body front and back. For head, Overcast all but side edges, then Whipstitch side edges together.

4. Using photo as a guide through step 6, Overlap two holes of body side edges, then glue to secure. Glue twig legs in body holes.

5. For tail, thread a 3-inch length of brown yarn through a top center hole along back edge; tie in a knot close to edge, then slightly unravel ends. Trim to desired length. Glue body back in body hole under tail.

6. Center and glue neck twig, just under top edge of front opening, then glue in body front.

7. Glue head over other end of twig neck. Glue twig antlers near top back edge of head. ✂

Design by
Lee Lindeman

COLOR KEY

Plastic Canvas Yarn	Yards
■ Brown #15	10

Color number given is for Uniek Needloft plastic canvas yarn.

Reindeer Front & Back
5 holes x 5 holes
Cut 2

Top Edge

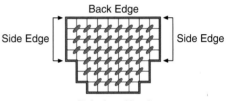

Reindeer Head
9 holes x 7 holes
Cut 1

Back Edge
Side Edge   Side Edge

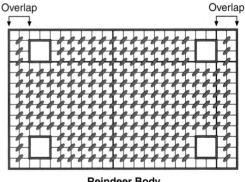

Reindeer Body
22 holes x 13 holes
Cut 1

Overlap   Overlap

Tiny Treasures Ornaments

Skill Level

Intermediate

Size

Ice Skater: 3¾ inches W x 4¾ inches H

Santa: 3¾ inches W x 4⅜ inches

This pair of engaging ornaments is sure to please you! A sweet skater and a jumping Santa will add a festive touch to your tree!

Designs by Lee Lindeman

Materials

Each Ornament
- ⅓ sheet 7-count plastic canvas
- Coats & Clark Red Heart Classic worsted weight yarn Art. E267 as listed in color key
- #3 pearl cotton as listed in color key
- #18 tapestry needle
- Small amount of polyester fiberfill
- Fine gold metallic cord
- Tacky craft glue or hot-glue gun

Ice Skater
- Metallic yarn or craft cord as listed in color key
- Fine silver metallic cord
- Small piece red felt or imitation suede
- Mini curly jute hair

Santa
- Small amount red felt
- Small amount white Rainbow plush felt from Kunin Felt

Ice Skater

1. Cut plastic canvas according to graphs (pages 165 and 167).

2. Overcast skates. Stitch front and back, working uncoded areas with black Continental Stitches.

3. When background stitching is completed, use black pearl cotton to work French Knot eyes; use pink yarn to work French Knot nose.

4. Whipstitch front and back together following graphs, stuffing with a small amount fiberfill before closing.

5. Thread desired length of fine gold cord through hole at top of skater's head. Tie ends in a knot to form a loop for hanging. Place knot close to head and add a dot of glue to secure.

6. Cut curly jute hair in short lengths; glue over tan stitching on skater's head for hair. Tie a small bow of silver metallic yarn and glue to center of hair on front.

7. Using pattern given, cut one skirt from red felt or imitation suede; also cut one ¼-inch-wide x 4½-inch-long strip for scarf. Fringe ends with scissors; wrap around neck and secure with glue. Glue skirt around waist, overlapping straight edges about ¼ inch at center back and gluing them together.

8. Glue skate A to bottom of skater's foot on the right and skate B to bottom of foot on the left. Thread fine silver cord through front edge of each skate boot; knot cord and tie in a bow. Secure bow with a dot of glue; trim cord ends.

Santa

1. Cut plastic canvas according to graphs.

2. Stitch pieces following graphs, working uncoded areas with jockey red Continental Stitches.

3. When background stitching is completed, use black pearl cotton to work French Knot eyes. Using white yarn, add Loop Stitches for beard and hair along sides of face, bottom of chin and on back of head; do not clip loops.

4. Whipstitch front and back together following graphs, stuffing with a small amount fiberfill before closing.

5. Thread desired length of fine gold cord through hole at top of hat. Tie ends in a knot to form a loop for hanging. Place knot close to head and add a dot of glue to secure.

6. From plush white felt, cut three ¼-inch circles for two buttons and one pompom for tip of hat; glue in place. To cover white areas, also cut ⅜-inch-wide strips to fit around coat cuffs, tops of boots, just below waist and around brim of hat; glue in place, butting ends neatly on back of ornament.

7. From red felt, cut a ⅛-inch circle for nose; glue in place. For mustache, tie a simple overhand knot in the center of a short piece of white yarn; trim yarn ends to ⅛ inch and glue knot to face below nose. ✂

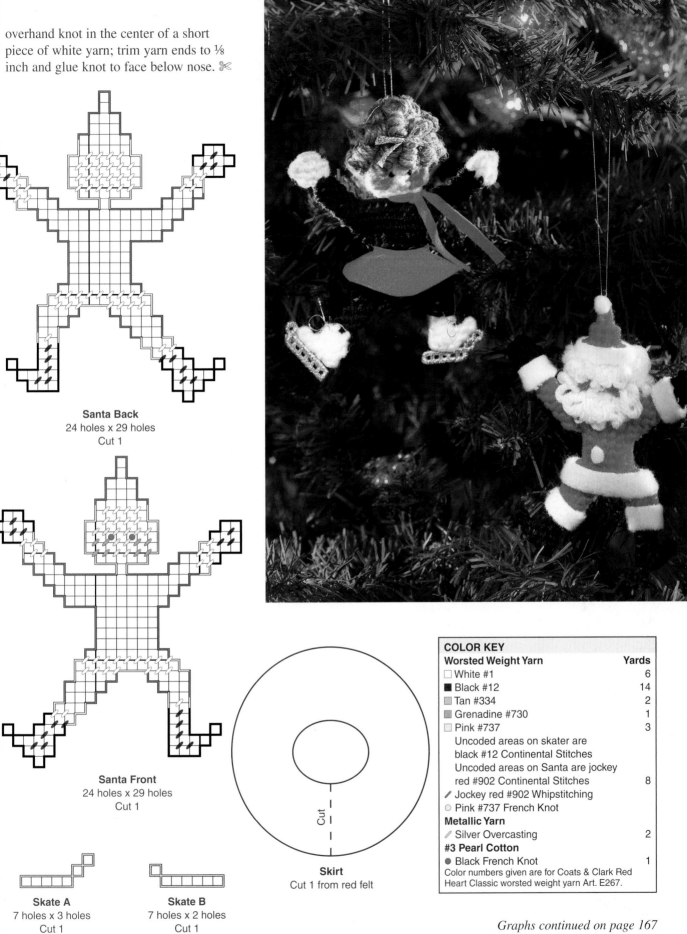

Santa Back
24 holes x 29 holes
Cut 1

Santa Front
24 holes x 29 holes
Cut 1

Skate A
7 holes x 3 holes
Cut 1

Skate B
7 holes x 2 holes
Cut 1

Cut

Skirt
Cut 1 from red felt

COLOR KEY

Worsted Weight Yarn	Yards
☐ White #1	6
■ Black #12	14
☐ Tan #334	2
▨ Grenadine #730	1
☐ Pink #737	3
Uncoded areas on skater are black #12 Continental Stitches	
Uncoded areas on Santa are jockey red #902 Continental Stitches	8
✐ Jockey red #902 Whipstitching	
○ Pink #737 French Knot	
Metallic Yarn	
⫽ Silver Overcasting	2
#3 Pearl Cotton	
● Black French Knot	1

Color numbers given are for Coats & Clark Red Heart Classic worsted weight yarn Art. E267.

Graphs continued on page 167

Gingerbread Girl Towel Topper

Skill Level

Beginner

Size

7⅞ inches W x 6½ inches H, excluding towel and ribbon

Cute as a button, this bright-eyed gingerbread girl will add sugar and spice to your holiday baking!

Materials

- ½ sheet 7-count plastic canvas
- Uniek Needloft plastic canvas yarn as listed in color key
- #3 pearl cotton as listed in color key
- #16 tapestry needle
- 2 (⅜-inch) black shank buttons
- 2 (⁵⁄₁₆-inch) red buttons
- 3¼ inches snap tape
- Dish towel in coordinating colors
- 30 inches ⅜-inch-wide red picot-edge satin ribbon
- 36 inches ³⁄₁₆-inch-wide red picot-edge satin ribbon
- Hand-sewing needle and sewing thread
- Fabric glue

Instructions

1. Cut plastic canvas according to graph.

2. Stitch piece following graph, working uncoded areas with maple Continental Stitches.

3. When background stitching is completed, work embroidery with black pearl cotton. Work eggshell Turkey Loop Stitches, making loops approximately 1-inch long.

COLOR KEY	
Plastic Canvas Yarn	**Yards**
■ Red #01	3
▨ Maple #13	15
▦ Holly #27	3
□ Eggshell #39	5
Uncoded areas are maple #13 Continental Stitches	
○ Eggshell #39 Turkey Loop Stitch	
#3 Pearl Cotton	
✐ Black Backstitch and Straight Stitch	1
● Attach black button	
✕ Attach red button	
● Attach hanger	
Color numbers given are for Uniek Needloft plastic canvas yarn.	

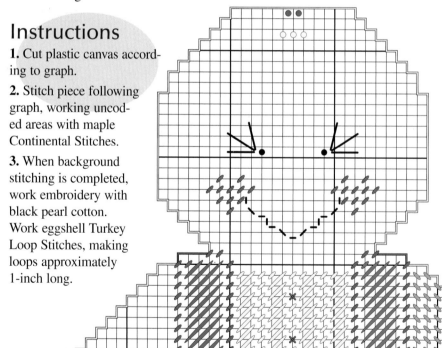

Gingerbread Girl
52 holes x 44 holes
Cut 1

Design by
Susan Leinberger

4. For eyes, sew black buttons to topper with black pearl cotton. Use one strand red yarn to attach red buttons where indicated on graph.

5. For hanger, thread ends of 3/16-inch-wide red ribbon from front to back where indicated on graph. Tie ends in a bow to form a loop for hanging.

6. Make a multiloop bow with 3/8-inch-wide ribbon and glue to top of head above Turkey Loop Stitches.

7. Cut towel in half. *Note: Only one half will be used in this project.*

8. Using hand-sewing needle and sewing thread, run a gathering stitch 1/4 inch from cut end of towel. Pull thread to gather towel to 3 1/4 inches; fasten off.

9. Glue one side of snap tape to gathered end of towel front. Glue remaining side of tape to back of girl, about 3/8 inch from bottom edge. Allow to dry, then fasten towel to base. ✂

Tiny Treasures Ornaments

Continued from page 165

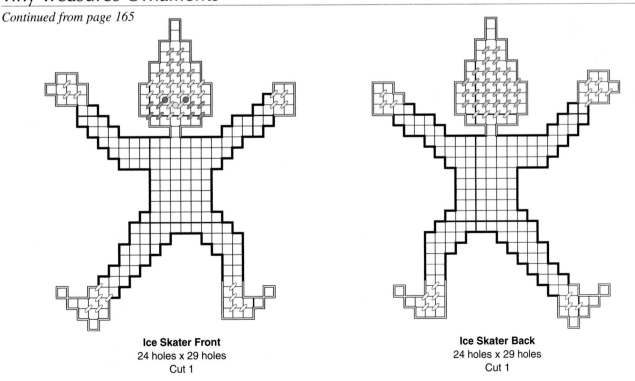

Ice Skater Front
24 holes x 29 holes
Cut 1

Ice Skater Back
24 holes x 29 holes
Cut 1

Candy Cane Pockets Tissue Topper

Skill Level
Beginner

Size
Fits boutique-style tissue box

Tiny candy canes peek out from the pockets of this cheery tissue topper, hinting at the goodies and presents that Santa will soon bring!

Design by
Joan Green

Materials
- 1½ sheets 7-count plastic canvas
- Coats & Clark Red Heart Super Saver worsted weight yarn Art. E301 as listed in color key
- ⅛ inch-wide Plastic Canvas 7 Metallic Needlepoint Yarn by Rainbow Gallery as listed in color key
- Arctic Rays Wispy Fringe by Rainbow Gallery as listed in color key
- Faux Fur furry singles yarn by Rainbow Gallery as listed in color key
- #16 tapestry needle
- 12 (2-inch long) plastic candy canes

Project Note
Stitch white portions of borders with one strand each of white wispy fringe and white furry singles yarn held together to make one working strand.

Instructions
1. Cut plastic canvas according to graphs.

2. Stitch pieces following graphs, working uncoded background on pockets and uncoded area on top with green metallic yarn Continental Stitches. Green pocket area on sides should remain unstitched.

3. When background stitching is completed, work red Backstitches on pockets and gold French Knots on sides and top.

4. Overcast inside edges on top with gold.

5. Using paddy green yarn throughout, Overcast top edges of pockets. Whipstitch one pocket to each side where indicated.

6. Using red throughout, Overcast bottom edges of sides. Whipstitch sides together, then Whipstitch sides to top.

7. Place three candy canes inside each pocket. ✂

COLOR KEY

Worsted Weight Yarn	Yards
■ Paddy green #368	32
☐ Emerald green #676	32

⅛-Inch Metallic Needlepoint Yarn

■ Red #PC5	20
Uncoded areas are green	
#PC4 Continental Stitches	10
✎ Gold #PC1 Overcasting	6
✏ Red #PC5 Backstitch	
○ Gold #PC1 French Knot	

Wispy Fringe & Furry Singles Yarn

☐ White #AR2 and White #FF1	10 each

Color numbers given are for Coats & Clark Red Heart Super Saver worsted weight yarn Art. E 301 and Rainbow Gallery Plastic Canvas 7 Metallic Needlepoint Yarn, Arctic Rays Wispy Fringe and Faux Fur furry singles yarn.

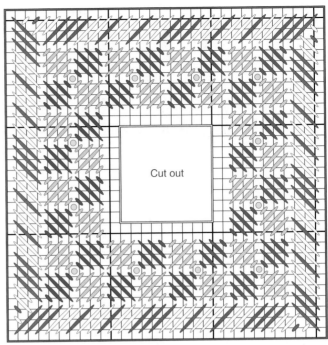

Candy Cane Pockets Topper Top
31 holes x 31 holes
Cut 1

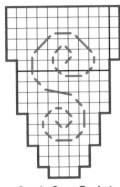

Candy Cane Pocket
11 holes x 16 holes
Cut 4

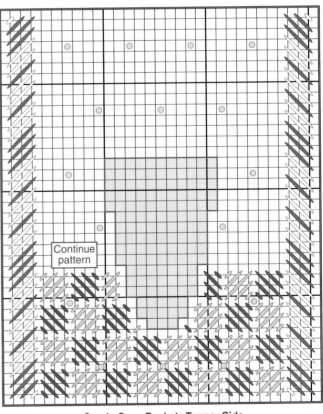

Candy Cane Pockets Topper Side
31 holes x 37 holes
Cut 4

Winter Cheer **169**

Puppy-Play Ornament

Skill Level
Beginner

Size
5 inches W x
5 inches H

This eager pup knows just how to open his present, and can't wait until Christmas!

Design by
Kathy Wirth

Materials
- ½ sheet 7-count plastic canvas
- Coats & Clark Red Heart Classic worsted weight yarn Art. E267 as listed in color key
- 4mm GlissenGloss Braid Ribbon 4 by Source Marketing
- 6-strand embroidery floss as listed in color key
- #16 tapestry needle
- ½ sheet self-adhesive Presto felt from Kunin Felt in desired color
- 2 (10-inch) lengths ¼-inch-wide red satin ribbon
- ¾-inch gold heart charm
- 2 black E beads
- Hot-glue gun

Cutting & Stitching
1. Cut plastic canvas according to graphs.
2. Trace puppy body on paper side of self-adhesive felt; cut out slightly smaller all around. Set aside.
3. Stitch pieces following graphs. When background stitching is completed, use 6 strands black floss to work Backstitches and Straight Stitches on muzzle, body and paw.

Assembly
1. Using gold braid ribbon, attach charm to body where indicated on graph.
2. Overcast top edges of muzzle from dot to dot; Overcast paw around bottom and right edges, and part of top edge from dot to dot.
3. Glue one end of one ribbon length to bottom backside of gift; wrap around bottom edge and bring ribbon up across front to unstitched canvas at top of gift; glue in place.
4. Match edges and Whipstitch unstitched portion of paw to body; glue paw over ribbon.
5. Matching edges throughout, Whipstitch unstitched portion of muzzle to head, then Whipstitch unstitched portion of head to body. Overcast remaining edges of body.
6. Thread gift ribbon from front to back through mouth at lefthand hole indicated on muzzle graph then from back to front at righthand hole indicated. Trim end diagonally.
7. Fold remaining ribbon length in half; glue ends to center top of ornament, forming a hanging loop. Remove paper from self-adhesive felt and adhere to back of body.
8. Glue seed beads to head for eyes as in photo. ✄

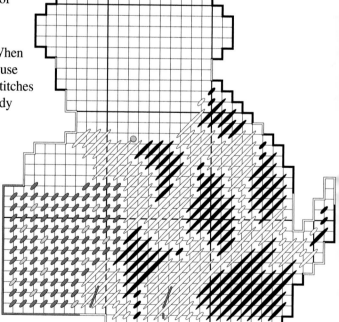

Puppy Body
32 holes x 32 holes
Cut 1

COLOR KEY

Worsted Weight Yarn	Yards
☐ White #1	8
■ Black #12	6
▨ Paddy green #686	3
4mm Metallic Braid Ribbon	
☐ Gold #01	1
6-Strand Embroidery Floss	
╱ Black Backstitch and Straight Stitch	1
● Attach charm	
● Attach ribbon	

Color numbers given are for Coats & Clark Red Heart Classic worsted weight yarn Art. E267 and GlissenGloss Braid Ribbon 4 by Source Marketing.

Puppy Head
19 holes x 15 holes
Cut 1

Puppy Paw
7 holes x 5 holes
Cut 1

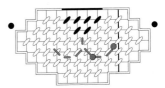

Puppy Muzzle
13 holes x 7 holes
Cut 1

Winter Bear Tote

Skill Level

Beginner

Size

8 inches W x 8¾ inches H x 4⅜ inches D

Decked out in his favorite striped sweater and warm scarf, this adorable bear is ready for an afternoon of skiing!

Design by
Michele Wilcox

Materials

- 3 sheets 7-count plastic canvas
- Uniek Needloft plastic canvas yarn as listed in color key
- #3 pearl cotton as listed in color key
- #16 tapestry needle
- 1 yard thin cotton rope

Instructions

1. Cut two sides and one each of front, back and bottom from plastic canvas according to graphs (pages 173 and 175).

2. Stitch pieces following graphs, working uncoded sky on front with royal Continental Stitches and stitching back completely with royal and white Diagonal Scotch Stitch pattern.

3. When background stitching is completed, use black pearl cotton to Backstitch ski pole and bear's smile, and add French Knot eyes and nose to bear.

4. Overcast openings for handles on front as graphed; Overcast openings on back with royal.

5. Using red, Whipstitch front and back to sides, then Whipstitch front, back and sides to bottom; Overcast top edges.

6. For handles, cut rope in half. Knot one end of one piece. Thread other end from front to back through one hole in tote front, then from back to front through other hole in tote front; knot end to hold handle in place. Repeat with remaining piece of rope to add handle to tote back. ✂

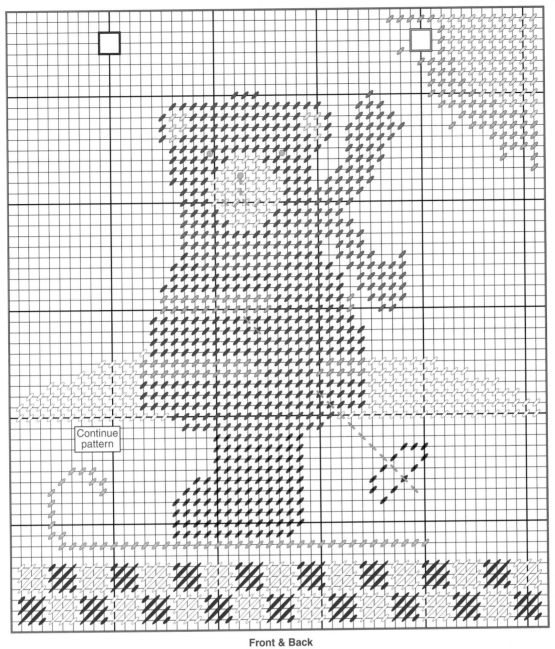

Continue
pattern

Front & Back
52 holes x 58 holes
Cut 2
Stitch front as graphed
Stitch back completely in
royal and white Scotch Stitches

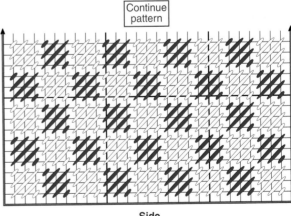

Continue
pattern

Side
28 holes 58 holes
Cut 2

COLOR KEY

Plastic Canvas Yarn	Yards
■ Black #00	3
■ Red #01	8
□ Pink #07	1
■ Tangerine #11	2
■ Maple #13	2
■ Cinnamon #14	5
■ Royal #32	65
□ Beige #40	1
□ White #41	65
■ Mermaid #53	4
□ Yellow #57	2

Uncoded sky area on front is
royal #32 Continental Stitches

#3 Pearl Cotton

✎ Black Backstitch	2
● Black French Knot	

Color numbers given are for Uniek Needloft
plastic canvas yarn.

Graphs continued on page 175

Winter Block Calendar

Skill Level
Beginner

Size
9⅞ inches W x
4⅛ inches H x
1⅞ inches D

Two little snowmen stand ready to mark off the fun-filled days of the season!

Design by
Angie Arickx

Materials
- 1 sheet 7-count plastic canvas
- Uniek Needloft plastic canvas yarn as listed in color key
- #16 tapestry needle
- Hot-glue gun

Project Note
Some graphs are shared with similar calendars in the other chapters of this book. Colors used for each season are given with the graphs and/or the instructions for that season.

Instructions
1. Following graphs throughout, cut fence, box long side, box short sides, box back and day blocks (pages 33 and 34); cut snowmen, snowflakes and month blocks.

2. Cut one 17-hole x 9-hole piece for month block side and two 9-hole x 9-hole pieces for month block ends; stitch all three pieces with red Continental Stitches.

3. Stitch and Overcast fence, snowmen and snowflakes, working uncoded areas on snowmen with white Continental Stitches. Stitch remaining pieces, working uncoded areas on block pieces with red Continental Stitches. Uncoded area on box back should remain unstitched.

4. Work French Knots on snowmen when background stitching is completed. Overcast one long edge of each box side.

5. Using red through step 7, Whipstitch box back to remaining long edges of box sides, then Whipstitch box long sides to box short sides.

6. Whipstitch the four month block sides together along long edges, then Whipstitch month block ends to sides.

7. For each day block, Whipstitch six pieces together, making sure there is one each of numbers "0", "1" and "2" with each block.

8. Making sure bottom edges are even, center and glue box back to fence, and snowmen to fence on each side of box. Glue snowflakes to fence above box. Place month and day blocks in box. ✂

COLOR KEY
Plastic Canvas Yarn	Yards
■ Black #00	2
■ Red #01	43
■ Christmas green #28	1
□ White #41	15
Camel #43	18
■ Bright orange #58	1
Uncoded areas on block pieces are red #01 Continental Stitches	
Uncoded areas on snowmen are white #41 Continental Stitches	
● Black #00 French Knot	
Color numbers given are for Uniek Needloft plastic canvas yarn.	

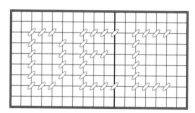

December Block Side
17 holes x 9 holes
Cut 1

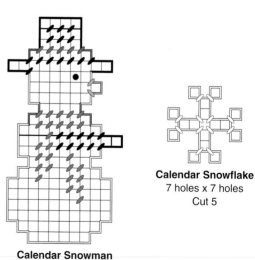

Calendar Snowman
11 holes x 21 holes
Cut 2, reverse 1

Calendar Snowflake
7 holes x 7 holes
Cut 5

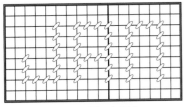

January Block Side
17 holes x 9 holes
Cut 1

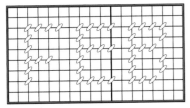

February Block Side
17 holes x 9 holes
Cut 1

Winter Bear Tote

Continued from page 173

Continued from page 173

COLOR KEY

Plastic Canvas Yarn	Yards
■ Black #00	3
■ Red #01	8
□ Pink #07	1
▨ Tangerine #11	2
▨ Maple #13	2
■ Cinnamon #14	5
■ Royal #32	65
□ Beige #40	1
□ White #41	65
■ Mermaid #53	4
▨ Yellow #57	2
Uncoded sky area on front is royal #32 Continental Stitches	

#3 Pearl Cotton

╱ Black Backstitch	2
● Black French Knot	

Color numbers given are for Uniek Needloft plastic canvas yarn.

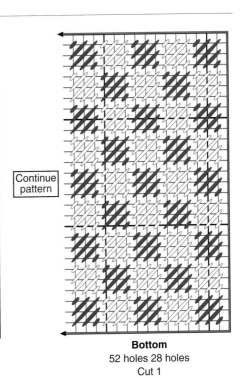

Continue pattern

Bottom
52 holes 28 holes
Cut 1

Dapper Snowman Centerpiece

Skill Level
Intermediate

Size
7½ W x 13½ inches H

This debonair snowman is a perfect gentleman, ready to help you with your winter decorating!

Design by Joan Green

Materials
- 2 sheets 7-count plastic canvas
- Coats & Clark Red Heart Classic worsted weight yarn Art. E267 as listed in color key
- Coats & Clark Red Heart Super Saver worsted weight yarn Art. E300 as listed in color key
- ⅛ inch-wide Plastic Canvas 7 Metallic Needlepoint Yarn by Rainbow Gallery as listed in color key
- Arctic Rays Wispy Fringe by Rainbow Gallery as listed in color key
- #16 tapestry needle
- 21 (4mm) pearl beads
- Hand-sewing needle and white thread
- 7½-inch white doll stand
- White self-adhesive Presto felt from Kunin Felt

Project Note
Stitch "snow" portions of snowman with one strand each of white worsted weight yarn and white wispy fringe held together to make one working strand.

Instructions
1. Cut plastic canvas according to graph. Cut one piece self-adhesive felt slightly smaller all around than snowman; set aside.

2. Snowman back will remain unstitched. Stitch snowman front following graphs, working uncoded areas with black yarn Continental Stitches.

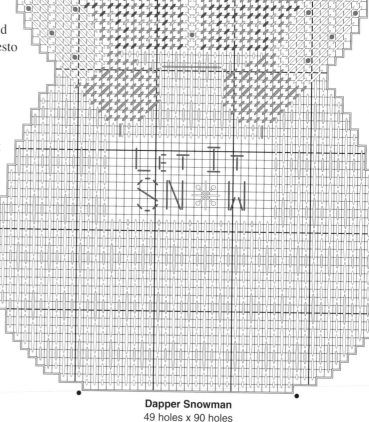

Dapper Snowman
49 holes x 90 holes
Cut 2, stitch 1

3. When background stitching is completed, embroider mouth, hanger for sign, and lettering on sign.

4. Using hand-sewing needle and white sewing thread, attach pearl beads where indicated on graph, knotting ends and weaving in securely.

5. Overcast bottom edge of front between black dots.

6. Adhere white felt to backside of stitched front piece, making sure edges are free for Whipstitching, then Whipstitch front and back together around side and top edges.

7. Discard ring portion of doll stand. Slip snowman over doll stand. ✄

COLOR KEY	
Worsted Weight Yarn & Wispy Fringe	**Yards**
☐ White #1 and white #AR2	28 each
Worsted Weight Yarn	
☐ Copper #289	1
☐ Raspberry #375	1
Uncoded area are black	
#12 Continental Stitches	6
╱ White #1 Backstitch and	
Straight Stitch	
╱ Black #12 Backstitch and	
Straight Stitch	
⅛-Inch Metallic Needlepoint Yarn	
☐ Gold #PC1	5
☐ White pearl #PC10	8
■ Black #PC11	8
▨ Fuchsia #PC13	10
▨ Forest green #PC17	8
Wispy Fringe	
○ White #AR2 French Knot	
● Attach pearl bead	

Color numbers given are for Coats & Clark Red Heart Classic worsted weight yarn Art. E267 and Super Saver worsted weight yarn Art. E300, and Rainbow Gallery Plastic Canvas 7 Metallic Needlepoint Yarn and Arctic Rays Wispy Fringe.

Smiling Snowflake

Skill Level
Beginner

Size
3¾ inches W x
3¾ inches H

With his winning smile and rosy pink cheeks, this frosted friend adds a fresh sense of fun for the holidays!

Materials
- 2 Uniek QuickShape plastic canvas hexagons
- ⅛-inch-wide Plastic Canvas 7 Metallic Needlepoint Yarn by Rainbow Gallery as listed in color key
- 6-strand embroidery floss as listed in color key
- #22 tapestry needle
- 2 (9mm) round pink cabochons from The Beadery
- White craft glue
- Hot-glue gun

Text continued on page 185

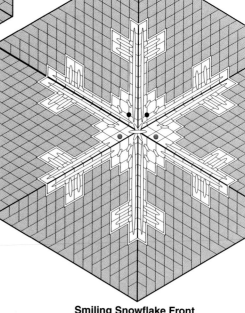

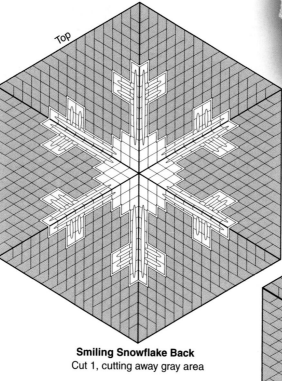

Smiling Snowflake Back
Cut 1, cutting away gray area

COLOR KEY

⅛-Inch Metallic Needlepoint Yarn	Yards
□ Snow #PC25	11
6-Strand Embroidery Floss	
● Black French Knot	1

Color number given is for Rainbow Gallery Plastic Canvas 7 Metallic Needlepoint Yarn.

Design by
Kathy Wirth

Smiling Snowflake Front
Cut 1, cutting away gray area

Snow Angel Coaster Set

Materials

- 1 sheet 7-count plastic canvas
- Coats & Clark Red Heart Super Saver worsted weight yarn Art. E300 as listed in color key
- Kreinik ⅛-inch ribbon as listed in color key
- DMC 6-strand embroidery floss as listed in color key
- #16 tapestry needle
- Small pebbles, rice or other weighted material

Instructions

1. Cut plastic canvas according to graphs (pages 180 and 181). Holder back, sides, bottom and support pieces will remain unstitched.

2. Stitch and Overcast coasters, working uncoded background with light teal Continental Stitches. Work silver ribbon Backstitches when background stitching and Overcasting are completed.

3. Stitch snowman following graph, working uncoded area with white yarn Continental Stitches. Do not Overcast edges.

4. Work black yarn Straight Stitches for eyes, then grass green Lazy Daisy Stitches. Next work skipper blue Bullion Knots (see diagram on page 181), working them in a curve as on graph and tacking down where indicated. Work light teal French Knots, wrapping yarn three times around needle.

5. Using 6 plies floss, work white French Knots for eye highlights and black French Knots for mouth, wrapping floss around needle three times. Work cornflower blue Backstitches with 3 plies floss.

Assembly

1. For holder, follow graphs and assembly diagram throughout assembly. Whipstitch center support to holder bottom at pink line. Whipstitch one short edge of each side piece and top edge of center support together through all three thicknesses.

2. Whipstitch back piece to bottom. Whipstitch front edge of bottom piece to bottom edge of snowman from dot to dot, Overcasting remaining bottom edges of snowman while Whipstitching.

3. Whipstitch bottom edges of sides to side edges of bottom, filling with pebbles, rice or other weighting material before closing. Tack sides to back in about every third or fourth hole.

4. Whipstitch one side support to side edges at bottom left of snowman and to side edges at bottom of back piece. Tack remaining side support to backside of snowman at blue line, then Whipstitch to side edges at bottom on other side of back piece.

5. Place coasters in holder as in photo to look like snowman's wings. ✂

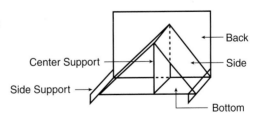

Assembly Diagram

Design by
Debbie Tabor

Skill Level

Intermediate

Size

5¾ inches W x
5¼ inches H x
1 inch D

This sweet angelic snowman has four crystal snowflakes to help watch over your table this winter!

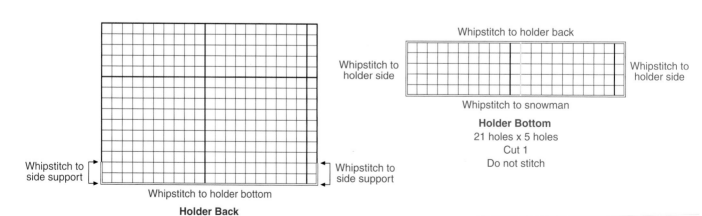

Whipstitch to holder back

Whipstitch to
holder side

Whipstitch to
holder side

Whipstitch to snowman

Holder Bottom
21 holes x 5 holes
Cut 1
Do not stitch

Whipstitch to
side support

Whipstitch to
side support

Whipstitch to holder bottom

Holder Back
21 holes x 15 holes
Cut 1
Do not stitch

COLOR KEY

Worsted Weight Yarn	Yards
☐ Petal pink #373	1
■ Hot red #390	2
Uncoded areas on snowman are white #311 Continental Stitches	1
Uncoded areas on coasters are light teal #355 Continental Stitches	11
∕ White #311 Overcasting and Whipstitching	30
∕ Light teal #355 Overcasting	
∕ Black #312 Backstitch and Straight Stitch	
⊅ Grass green #687 Lazy Daisy Stitch	1
∪ Skipper blue #384 Bullion Knot	1
● Light teal #355 French Knot	
⅛-Inch Ribbon	
∕ Silver #001 Backstitch	18
6-Strand Embroidery Floss	
∕ Cornflower blue #3807 (3-ply) Backstitch	2
● Black #310 (6-ply) French Knot	1
○ White #1001 (6-ply) French Knot	1

Color numbers given are for Coats & Clark Red Heart Super Saver worsted weight yarn Art. E300, Kreinik ⅛-inch Ribbon and DMC 6-strand embroidery floss.

Bring yarn up at 1, down at 2, leaving a loop of yarn.

Bring needle up again at 1, but do not pull through canvas. Wrap yarn around needle a few times, keeping first wrap next to plastic canvas.

Holding wraps in place, pull needle and yarn completely through wrapped yarn, keeping the curved shape. Then bring needle down again at 2 to anchor knot. Tack down at middle of curve.

Bullion Knot

Whipstitch to center support and other holder side ← → Whipstitch to holder bottom

Holder Side
15 holes x 5 holes
Cut 2
Do not stitch

Whipstitch to snowman ← → Whipstitch to holder back

Holder Side Support
8 holes x 2 holes
Cut 2
Do not stitch

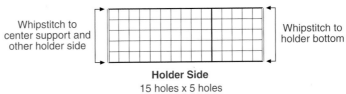

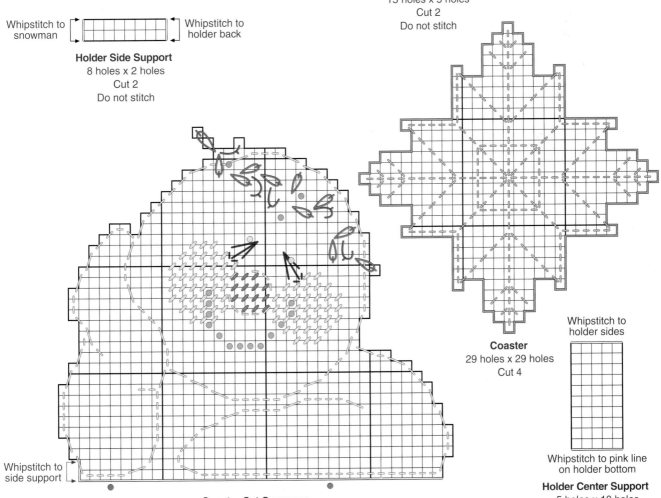

Coaster
29 holes x 29 holes
Cut 4

Coaster Set Snowman
38 holes x 33 holes
Cut 1

Whipstitch to side support

Whipstitch to holder sides

Whipstitch to pink line on holder bottom

Holder Center Support
5 holes x 10 holes
Cut 1
Do not stitch

Angel in My Pocket

Skill Level
Beginner

Size
Pocket: 3¼ inches
W x 3⅞ inches H,
excluding hanger

Teddy Angel:
3⅛ inches W x
4⅝ inches H

Stitch this simple and quick guardian angel bear to watch over your smallest loved one!

Design by
Vicki Blizzard

Materials
- 1 sheet 7-count plastic canvas
- Uniek Needloft plastic canvas yarn as listed in color key
- ⅛-inch-wide Plastic Canvas 7 Metallic Needlepoint Yarn by Rainbow Gallery as listed in color key
- #3 pearl cotton as listed in color key
- #16 tapestry needle
- 2 (5mm) round black cabochons
- 10 inches heavyweight natural jute
- Jewel glue
- Hot-glue gun

Instructions
1. Cut plastic canvas according to graphs.

2. Stitch and Overcast halo. Stitch one bear body as graphed for front; stitch remaining body completely in maple Continental Stitches for back. Stitch remaining pieces following graphs, working uncoded background on pockets with dark royal Continental Stitches.

3. Work beige French Knots on body front for paws. Using light brown pearl cotton, Backstitch mouth and add French Knot nose to muzzle; add French Knot belly button to belly. Using bright red pearl cotton, add Backstitched trim to both pockets.

4. Overcast muzzle and belly with beige yarn. Whipstitch bear front and back together with maple. Whipstitch wings together with white.

5. Hot-glue muzzle and belly to front of bear; hot-glue halo to back of bear's head and wings to back of bear. Using jewel glue, attach cabochons for eyes.

6. Using dark royal, Overcast top edges of pockets; Whipstitch pockets together along remaining edges. Hot-glue ends of jute inside pocket at sides for handle.

7. Insert bear in pocket. ✂

COLOR KEY

Plastic Canvas Yarn		Yards
■	Maple #13	9
□	Beige #40	2
□	White #41	5
	Uncoded background on pockets are dark royal Continental Stitches #48	15
⁄	Dark royal #48 Overcasting and Whipstitching	
○	Beige #40 French Knot	
⅛-Inch Metallic Needlepoint Yarn		
□	Gold #PC1	1
#3 Pearl Cotton		
⁄	Bright red Backstitch	1
⁄	Light brown Backstitch	1
●	Light brown French Knot	

Color numbers given are for Uniek Needloft plastic canvas yarn and Rainbow Gallery Plastic Canvas 7 Metallic Needlepoint Yarn.

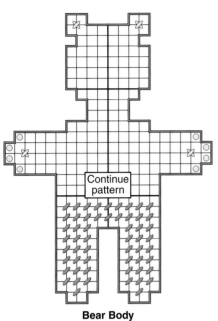

Bear Body
20 holes x 27 holes
Cut 2
Stitch 1 as shown for front
Stitch 1 completely in maple
Continental Stitches for back

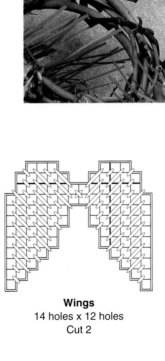

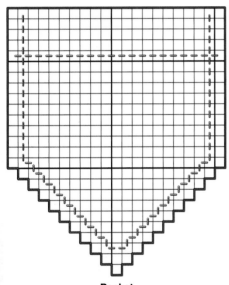

Pocket
21 holes x 25 holes
Cut 2

Muzzle
5 holes x 4 holes
Cut 1

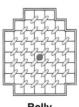

Wings
14 holes x 12 holes
Cut 2

Belly
7 holes x 8 holes
Cut 1

Halo
5 holes x 5 holes
Cut 1

Winter Cheer **183**

Angel Window Ornament

Skill Level
Beginner

Size
9¼ inches W x 5¾ inches H

Celebrate the holidays with the sweet innocence of these adorable little angels!

Materials
- ½ sheet 7-count plastic canvas
- Uniek Needloft plastic canvas yarn as listed in color key
- Kreinik Heavy (#32) Braid as listed in color key
- #3 pearl cotton as listed in color key
- DMC #5 pearl cotton as listed in color key
- DMC 6-strand embroidery floss as listed in color key
- #16 tapestry needle
- 18 inches fine metallic cord
- 3 silver liberty bells: small, medium and large
- Thick white glue

Instructions
1. Cut plastic canvas according to graph.

2. Stitch and Overcast piece following graph, working uncoded areas on banners with baby yellow Continental Stitches and uncoded areas on angels' robes with baby blue Continental Stitches.

3. When background stitching is completed, Backstitch halos and detail on robes with Vatican braid. Work Cross Stitches for cheeks with 2 plies light salmon.

4. Work remaining embroidery with pearl cotton, wrapping white #3 pearl cotton around needle twice for French Knots on robes; wrap #5 pearl cotton around needle one time for black French Knot eyes and for mauve French Knot dot on exclamation point.

Design by
Janelle Giese

5. Using white pearl cotton, cluster bells and sew to heart where indicated on graph. Tie a bow around bell attachment with Vatican braid; trim ends. Seal ends and secure bow with dabs of glue.

6. For hanger, thread ends of 18-inch length of fine metallic cord through holes indicated with arrows; tie knots just above top edge, adjusting hanger to desired height. ✂

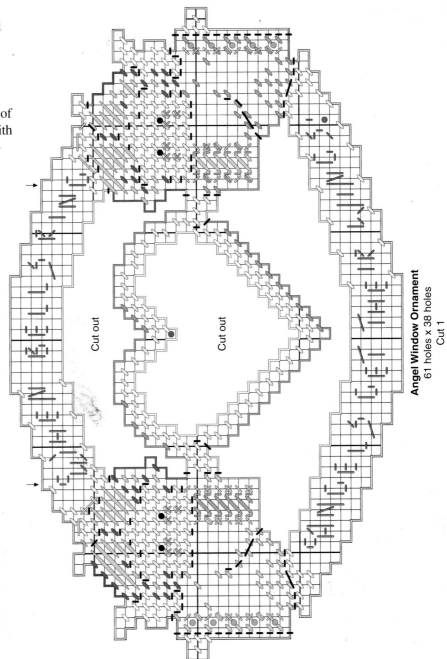

Angel Window Ornament
61 holes x 38 holes
Cut 1

Cut out

Cut out

COLOR KEY	
Plastic Canvas Yarn	**Yards**
▨ Lavender #05	2
☐ Pink #07	1
■ Cinnamon #15	2
▨ Moss #25	2
☐ White #41	3
▨ Camel #43	2
▨ Lilac #45	2
☐ Flesh tone #56	7
Uncoded areas on banners are baby yellow #21 Continental Stitches	6
Uncoded areas on robes are baby blue #36 Continental Stitches	3
Heavy (#32) Braid	
╱ Vatican #102HL Backstich and Overcasting	2
#3 Pearl Cotton	
╱ White Backstitch	2
● White French Knot	
#5 Pearl Cotton	
╱ Black #310 Backstitch and Straight Stitch	4
╱ Dark mauve #3685 Backstitch and and Straight Stitch	3
● Black #310 French Knot	
● Dark mauve #3685 French Knot	
6-Strand Embroidery Floss	
✕ Light Salmon #761 Cross Stitch	1
● Attach bells	
Color numbers given are for Uniek Needloft plastic canvas yarn, Kreinik Heavy (#32) Braid, and DMC #5 pearl cotton and 6-strand embroidery floss.	

Smiling Snowflake
Continued from page 178

Instructions

1. Cut plastic canvas according to graphs (page 178), cutting away gray areas.

2. Stitch and Overcast pieces following graphs, keeping yarn smooth and flat while stitching and leaving areas unstitched as shown.

3. When background stitching is completed, use 6 strands black floss to work mouth from red dot to red dot, allowing enough floss for a curved shape (see photo); work French Knots for eyes.

4. Hot-glue cabochons to unworked area on front, then spread small amount of white glue with finger on mouth to keep curved shape.

5. With right sides facing up, hot-glue center of front to back, placing arms of back snowflake between arms of front snowflake.

6. Thread desired length of metallic needlepoint yarn through top holes of snowflake. Ties ends together in a knot to form a loop for hanging. ✂

Valentine Hearts Tissue Topper

Skill Level
Intermediate

Size
Fits regular-size tissue box

Delicately detailed and sweet as candy, this Valentine confection will add love to any room!

Design by
Angie Arickx

Materials

- 2 sheets 7-count plastic canvas
- Uniek Needloft plastic canvas yarn as listed in color key
- #16 tapestry needle
- Hot-glue gun

Instructions

1. Cut plastic canvas according to graphs (pages 187 and 188).

2. Stitch pieces following graphs, working uncoded areas with white Continental Stitches.

3. Overcast hearts, lace pieces, inside edges of topper top and bottom edges of topper sides.

4. Whipstitch long sides to short sides with pink; Whipstitch sides to top with white.

5. Glue lace top pieces in place on topper top. Glue two lace long sides to each topper long side and two lace short sides to each topper short side, placing lacy edges toward the center (see photo).

6. Glue five hearts evenly spaced to long sides; glue three hearts evenly spaced to short sides. ✂

COLOR KEY	
Plastic Canvas Yarn	**Yards**
■ Lavender #05	26
☐ Pink #07	63
☐ White #41	71
Uncoded areas are white #41 Continental Stitches	
Color numbers given are for Uniek Needloft plastic canvas yarn.	

Outer Lace Top
65 holes x 35 holes
Cut 1

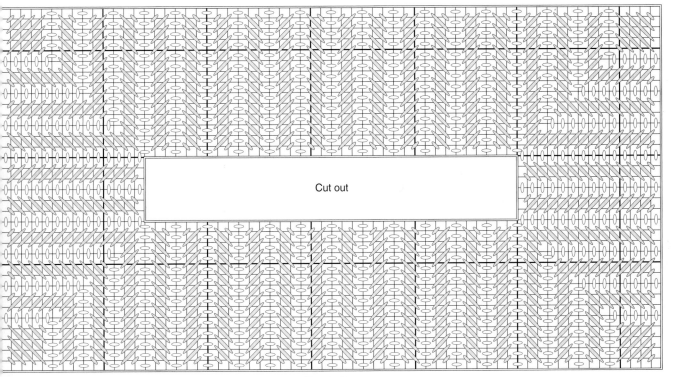

Topper Top
64 holes x 34 holes
Cut 1

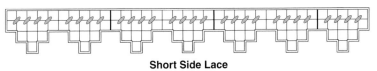

Short Side Lace
35 holes x 4 holes
Cut 2

Winter Cheer **187**

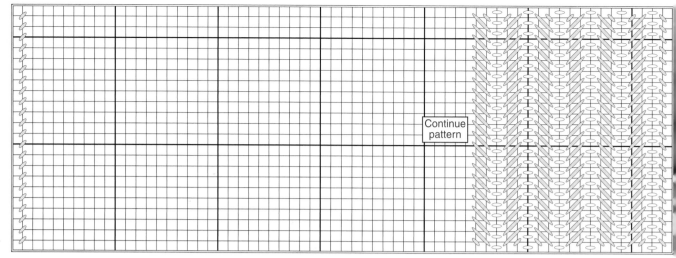

Topper Long Side
64 holes x 23 holes
Cut 2

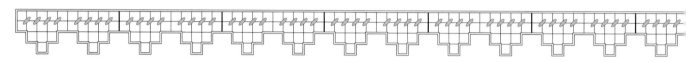

Long Side Lace
65 holes x 4 holes
Cut 2

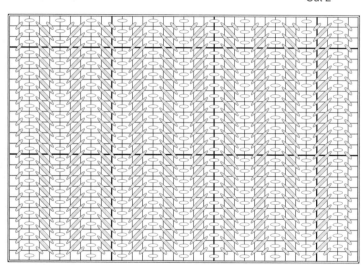

Topper Short Side
34 holes x 23 holes
Cut 2

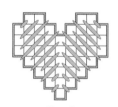

Heart
9 holes x 8 holes
Cut 16

COLOR KEY	
Plastic Canvas Yarn	**Yards**
▨ Lavender #05	26
▨ Pink #07	63
☐ White #41	71
Uncoded areas are white	
#41 Continental Stitches	
Color numbers given are for Uniek Needloft plastic canvas yarn.	

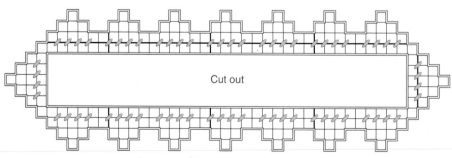

Center Lace Top
43 holes x 13 holes
Cut 1

Peek-a-Boo Teddy Pin

Materials

- Small amount 10-count plastic canvas
- DMC #3 pearl cotton as listed in color key
- 6-strand embroidery floss as listed in color key
- 11mm red heart bead
- 8-inches ⅛-inch-wide pink satin ribbon
- 1-inch pin back
- Hot-glue gun

Instructions

1. Cut plastic canvas according to graphs.

2. Stitch pieces following graphs, working uncoded areas with tan Continental Stitches. Overcast all but top edges of arms.

3. Use 6 strands floss to work French Knot eyes. Use 3 strands floss to work Straight Stitch for mouth; work French Knots at each end of mouth and on tummy for belly button.

4. Sew heart bead to teddy bear's tummy where indicated.

5. Whipstitch top edges of arms to bear's body where indicated. Attach legs to bottom of body where indicated with loops of light brown pearl cotton, allowing legs to dangle about ⅜-inch below body.

6. Tie ribbon in small bow; trim ends. Glue bow to base of bear's ear. Glue pin back to back of bear. ✂

Skill Level
Beginner

Size
1⁵⁄₁₆ inches W x 2⅞ inches H

Give a special friend a handstitched hug with this sweet teddy bear pin. Open her arms to see her love-filled heart!

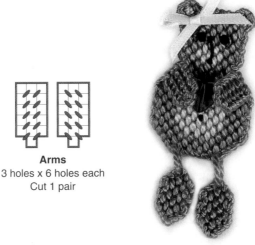

Arms
3 holes x 6 holes each
Cut 1 pair

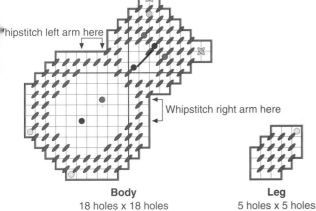

Whipstitch left arm here

Whipstitch right arm here

Body
18 holes x 18 holes
Cut 1

Leg
5 holes x 5 holes
Cut 2

COLOR KEY	
#3 Pearl Cotton	**Yards**
■ Light brown #434	4
☐ Tan #436	2
Uncoded areas are tan #436 Continental Stitches	
6-Strand Embroidery Floss	
✒ Black (3-strand) Straight Stitch	1
● Black (3-strand) French Knot	
● Black (6-strand) French Knot	
● Attach heart bead	
○ Attach leg	
○ Attach ribbon bow	
Color numbers given are for DMC #3 pearl cotton.	

Design by Vicki Blizzard

Stitch Guide

Use the following diagrams to expand your plastic canvas stitching skills. For each diagram, bring needle up through canvas at the red number one and go back down through the canvas at the red number two. The second stitch is numbered in green. Always bring needle up through the canvas at odd numbers and take it back down through the canvas at the even numbers.

Background Stitches

The following stitches are used for filling in large areas of canvas. The Continental Stitch is the most commonly used stitch. Other stitches, such as the Condensed Mosaic and Scotch Stitch, fill in large areas of canvas more quickly than the Continental Stitch because their stitches cover a larger area of canvas.

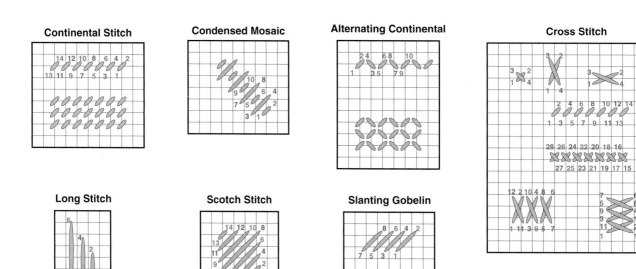

Embroidery Stitches

These stitches are worked on top of a stitched area to add detail to the project. Embroidery stitches are usually worked with one strand of yarn, several strands of pearl cotton or several strands of embroidery floss.

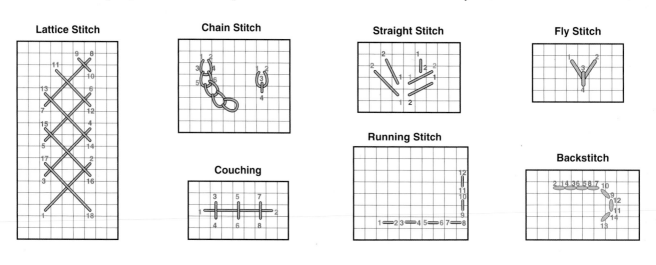

Embroidery Stitches

French Knot

Bring needle up through canvas.

Wrap yarn around needle 1 to 3 times, depending on desired size of knot; take needle back through canvas through same hole.

Lazy Daisy

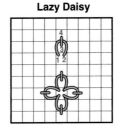

Bring yarn needle up through canvas, then back down in same hole, leaving a small loop.

Then, bring needle up inside loop; take needle back down through canvas on other side of loop.

Loop Stitch/Turkey Loop Stitch

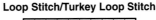

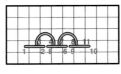

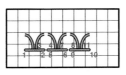

The top diagram shows this stitch left intact. This is an effective stitch for giving a project dimensional hair. The bottom diagram demonstrates the cut loop stitch. Because each stitch is anchored, cutting it will not cause the stitches to come out. A group of cut loop stitches gives a fluffy, soft look and feel to your project.

Specialty Stitches

The following stitches can be worked either on top of a previously stitched area or directly onto the canvas. Like the embroidery stitches, these too add wonderful detail and give your stitching additional interest and texture.

Diamond Eyelet

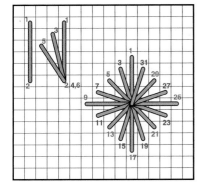

For each stitch, bring needle up at odd numbers and down through canvas at center hole.

Smyrna Cross

Satin Stitches

Finishing Stitches

Overcast/Whipstitch

Overcasting and Whipstitching are used to finish the outer edges of the canvas. Overcasting is done to finish one edge at a time. Whipstitching is used to stitch two or more pieces of canvas together along an edge. For both Overcasting and Whipstitching, work one stitch in each hole along straight edges and inside corners, and two or three stitches in outside corners.

Lark's Head Knot

The Lark's Head Knot is used for a fringe edge or for attaching a hanging loop.

Special Thanks

We would like to acknowledge and thank the following designers whose original work has been published in this collection. We appreciate and value their creativity and dedication to designing quality plastic canvas projects!

Debra Arch
"Franklin"stein, Prancer

Angie Arickx
Autumn Block Calendar, Harvest Bear Tissue Topper, Harvest Birdhouse, Spring Calendar, Summer Block Calendar, Sunflower Birdhouse, Valentine Hearts Tissue Topper, Winter Block Calendar

Eunice Asberry
Curious Kitten Coasters

Nancy Barrett
Country Apples

Nancy Billetdeaux
Gourds for Sale Coaster Set

Vicki Blizzard
Angel in My Pocket, Fruit Fairies, Peek-a-Boo Teddy Pin

Ronda Bryce
Butterfly & Flower Pokes, Gift Bear

Judy Collishaw
Cactus Kid Thermometer, Country Chicken Bucket, Little Penguin Napkin Ring

Mary T. Cosgrove
Sunflower Season Caddy & Candleholder

Carol Dace
Napkin Ring Blossoms

Nancy Dorman
Haunted House Tissue Topper

Susan D. Fisher
Nosy Bunny Tote

Janelle Giese
Angel Window Ornament, Autumn Kitties, Birdies Welcome, Bunnies Welcome, Cottage Clip, Cottage Planter, Fairy Ornaments, Gardener Frog Peg Rack, Kiss the Cook, Summer Kids Welcome, Winter Penguins

Joan Green
Birds of Beauty, Bunny Ornament, Candy Cane Pockets Tissue Topper, Dapper Snowman Centerpiece, Happy Birthday Hat, Wind Chime Birdhouse

Robin Howard-Will
Ghostly Greetings, Growing Patriots Flowerpot

Kathleen Hurley
Baby Leo Birthday Frame, Floral Baskets, Spring Chicks Basket

Patricia Klesh
Spooky Doorknob Hanger

Christina Laws
Uncle Sam Shelf Sitter

Susan Leinberger
Gingerbread Girl Towel Topper, Goofy Ghouls Magnet Trio, Mini Trinket Boxes

Lee Lindeman
Happy Clowns Centerpiece, Tabletop Reindeer, Tiny Treasures Ornaments

Nancy Marshall
Flower Frames Screen, Halloween Heads Party Favors, Pet Buddies, Turkey Farmer Wall Hanging

Debbie Tabor
Snow Angel Coaster Set

Michele Wilcox
Funky Chicken Tissue Topper, Happy Elf Door Hanger, Ladybug Basket, Summer Fling Wall Ornament, Winter Bear Tote

Kathy Wirth
Cinnamon Stick Snowman & Santa, Funky Bug Plaques, Puppy-Play Ornament, Smiling Snowflake, Soft Floral Tissue Topper, Tiger Kitty Tissue Topper, Welcome Friends Banner

Buyer's Guide

When looking for a specific material, first check your local craft and retail stores. If you are unable to locate a product locally, contact the manufacturers listed below for the closest retail source in your area or a mail-order source.

Amaco
American Art Clay Co. Inc.
4717 W. 16th St.
Indianapolis, IN 46222-2598
(317) 244-6871
www.amaco.com

The Beadery
P.O. Box 178
Hope Valley, RI 02832
(401) 539-2432

Coats & Clark
Consumer Service
P.O. Box 12229
Greenville, SC 29612-0229
(800) 648-1479
www.coatsandclark.com

Creative Co-op Inc.
4651 Hickory Hill Rd., Suite 101
Memphis, TN 38141
(901) 333-0133
www.creativecoop.com

Darice
Mail-order source:
Schrock's International
P.O. Box 538
Bolivar, OH 44612
(330) 874-3700

DMC Corp.
Hackensack Ave. Bldg. 10A
South Kearny, NJ 07032-4688
(800) 275-4117
www.dmc-usa.com

Fibre-Craft Materials Corp.
Mail-order source:
Kirchen Brothers
P.O. Box 1016
Skokie, IL 60076
(800) 378-5024
e-mail: www.kbcrafts.com

Gay Bowles Sales Inc.
P.O. Box 1060
Janesville, WI 53547
(800) 447-1332
www.millhill.com

Kreinik Mfg. Co. Inc.
3106 Timanus Ln., #101
Baltimore, MD 21244-2871
(800) 537-2166

Kunin Felt Co./Foss Mfg. Co. Inc.
P.O. Box 5000
Hampton, NH 03843-5000
(603) 929-6100
www.kuninfelt.com

Rainbow Gallery
7412 Fulton Ave., #5
North Hollywood, CA 91605-4126
www.rainbowgallery.com

Source Marketing
P.O. Box 9701
Michigan City, IN 46360-9701
(219) 873-1000
www.glissengloss.com

Uniek
Mail-order source:
Annie's Attic
1 Annie Ln.
Big Sandy, TX 75755
(800) 582-6643
www.anniesattic.com

Walnut Hollow Farm Inc.
1409 State Rd. 23
Dodgeville, WI 53533-2112
(800) 950-5101
www.walnuthollow.com